ENTERPRISE *in* LATIN AMERICA

Business Attitudes in a Developing Economy

ENTERPRISE *in* LATIN AMERICA

Business Attitudes in
a Developing Economy

By Albert Lauterbach

Sarah Lawrence College

CORNELL UNIVERSITY PRESS

Ithaca, New York

CORNELL UNIVERSITY PRESS

First published 1966

Library of Congress Catalog Card Number: 65-26087

PRINTED IN THE UNITED STATES OF AMERICA
BY THE VAIL-BALLOU PRESS, INC.

Acknowledgments

THE persons and organizations that have been helpful in the research leading to this publication are far too numerous to be listed. But I must emphasize, at least in a general way, my gratitude to all the cooperative and patient interviewees in various parts of Latin America, and to the individual experts, productivity centers, research institutes, and trade associations that have helped further this study in one way or another.

Much of the material was collected during my Brookings Research Professorship for 1962–1963, and I am much obliged to the Brookings Institution for this opportunity. Responsibility for the content of this book, of course, rests solely with the author.

v

Acknowledgments

Substantial sections of the book contain in a modified form materials published in the following journals:

Revista de Economía Latinoamericana, Caracas
Kyklos International Review for Social Sciences, Basle
Economie Appliquée, Paris
Industrial and Labor Relations Review, Ithaca, New York
Journal of Inter-American Studies, Coral Gables, Florida
Business History Review, Cambridge, Massachusetts

In addition, some of the findings entered into a memorandum written for the Organization of American States, Department of Economic Affairs. To all of these I am grateful for permitting the use of various materials contained in this book.

ALBERT LAUTERBACH

Bronxville, New York
March 1965

Contents

Contents

Introduction

ALTHOUGH business activities are often studied exclusively from an economic, financial, or administrative point of view, additional knowledge about the attitudes and motives of enterprise managers is indispensable. Unless psychological factors are taken into account in studying managerial behavior, there is a danger of serious errors regarding the regular or "normal" character of specific kinds of managerial decisions. In order to determine to what extent behavior patterns from the past, as summarized in statistical data, can be expected to continue in the future, it is essential to grasp the driving forces of economic actions: unconscious factors, the influence of personality, and the cultural characteristics of the population in which the managers are rooted.

The author has not assumed, of course, that the underlying attitudes of enterprise managers are necessarily realistic or well balanced, nor that their views alone should determine economic policy. The beliefs of labor and of population groups such as farmers and professionals are no less important. But the attitudes of enterprise managers unquestionably have a significant effect on the course of economic development, and knowledge of these attitudes can be especially helpful in relating the economic needs of newly developing areas to policy decisions at home and abroad.

Traditionally, thinking about the relationship between enterprise management and development needs in the poorer countries has very largely originated in the West. In areas of lagging development there has been, almost inevitably, little original thought on this subject, and some type of Western concept has invariably been adopted.

The varieties of Western interpretation can by and large be divided into the following four approaches (these are not mutually exclusive):

First, that based upon the belief that the essence of management is the same everywhere regardless of the stage of economic development. The organizational tasks that characterize enterprise management are not assumed to differ basically even though the external circumstances vary in regard to technology, educational level, capital supply, and public administration. Management in less developed areas, therefore, needs to strive to learn from the West and to catch up with it as quickly as possible. "Industrial man" will sooner or later take over in all the developing areas, and specifically in their managerial groups.

Second, that based upon the interpretation of economic

development essentially as "entrepreneurship," which is usually defined in terms of competitive readiness to innovate and to take risks. The decisive question here is seen to be how to arouse such a spirit where it has been characteristically absent. In the light of Western experience, élites or fringe groups such as ethnic or religious minorities are usually considered the most likely sources of the entrepreneurial spirit. A related question is *how* the process can best be speeded up through public or private action, including foreign assistance. The psychological variety of such neo-Schumpeterian thinking is focused either on the spread of a "need for achievement" among cultural and social groups or on the kinds of personality-forming influences that are conducive to the rise of an entrepreneurial mentality.

Third, an approach based upon emphasizing induced investment, especially within a framework of unbalanced economic growth that can open up new business opportunities. One possible implication of this approach is that effective enterprise management will result from the provision of suitable inducement mechanisms for investment rather than from reliance on a demonstration effect of Western managerial experience.

Fourth, an approach based upon relating the nature and functioning of management in a given area to the prevailing social system and cultural values both before and during a major development effort. Apart from purely technical requirements it is thus not assumed that there is only one set of "sound" management principles that can be applied in any area and period regardless of the timing, location, and phase of economic development. Rather, the specific attitudes and practices of management, as well as possible measures for its development, are put into the context of the sociocultural heritage of the area and the population involved. It is this approach that the author has been chiefly interested in and that he has attempted to implement through empirical investigation.

The present study is based to a considerable degree on explorations in Latin America, but also applies to some extent, I believe, to certain other parts of the world. We still need to determine what actually is to be interpreted as "development," in contrast to "change" in general or "growth"; we need to know more about what causes development and what exactly takes place when it occurs; we need to understand better how economic, political, psychological, and sociocultural factors interact in the process of development. The study of managerial attitudes in a specific part of the world may contribute something to our general knowledge. It is important to know, in particular, the extent to which enterprise managers in a newly developing area resemble managers in recent or earlier phases of Western European and North American economic history, and the extent to which the former group shows distinctive attitudinal traits compared to their counterparts in other areas of the world today.

I do not, of course, mean to imply that generalizations about Latin American managers are necessarily more valid than other generalizations about Latin America or any other major area. For the purposes of this study the differences of cultural background, political history, and economic development among the various areas of Latin America are no less interesting than the factors that do permit generalization.

Similarities between Latin American and Western European or North American management are often superficial. Office arrangements, organization charts, and even business

Introduction

terminology may often seem alike. But in his actual role in the company, and in his relations with employees, customers, suppliers, competitors, bankers, and politicians, the enterprise manager may be influenced strongly, if often unconsciously, by the feudal legacy of his society, by the Indian, Spanish, or Portuguese outlook on life, and by other cultural factors that are absent or weak in North America and Western Europe.

To obtain firsthand evidence concerning the attitudes of Latin American enterprise managers, the interview method was used extensively. In addition, much information was obtained from more informal conversations with businessmen; from attendance at meetings of management groups; from discussions with government officials, economists, and productivity experts with experience in the field of the investigation; and from the study of materials published or prepared by trade associations or individual companies in the countries concerned.

The first phase of the investigation consisted of a detailed study of managerial attitudes in one country—Chile. The results were published in 1961 by the Instituto de Economía, Universidad de Chile, Santiago, under the title *Managerial Attitudes in Chile* (Spanish version, *Las Actitudes Administrativas en Chile*). During 1959 and 1960 interviews were also held with enterprise managers in Colombia, Peru, Argentina, Uruguay, and Southern and Central Brazil, and a few more in Bolivia and Paraguay.[1] There fol-

[1] This phase of the investigation was discussed in the following publications: "Actitudes Empresariales y el Desarrollo Económico," *Revista de Economía Latinoamericana*, Caracas, Venezuela (June, 1961); "Managerial Attitudes and Economic Development," *Kyklos*, Basle, Switzerland, Vol. XV/2 (1962); "Comportements Économiques en Amérique Latine Occidentale," *Économie Appliquée*, Paris, France, Vol. XV/3 (1962).

lowed in 1962 and 1963 interviews with managers in Mexico, Guatemala, El Salvador, Venezuela, and Northeast Brazil. When a selected group of Chilean managers from the original sample was reinterviewed in 1963, it was interesting to discover that the conspicuous change in the economic and monetary situation in Chile had had very little effect on the personal attitudes of the interviewees.

The 1962–1963 questionnaire was somewhat different in form from the questionnaire that had been used three years earlier. Its first part focused on the interviewee's experience in his own enterprise. The second part was aimed at finding out his views regarding the economic development of the nation. The questionnaire, which was intended to provide a stimulating starting point for the interviews rather than a rigid framework, is given in Appendix 1. The nature of the data obtained is essentially qualitative. For this reason the tabulations of the answers, which were prepared for the author's use, were not included in the book version of this study, though some of them were used in the reviews listed in the Acknowledgments.

The total number of interviews with managers was 324, not counting more informal conversations with members of this group and another 79 interviews held with the non-managerial groups of experts mentioned earlier. Details regarding the sample appear in Appendixes 2 and 3. The monopolistic or localized character of many enterprises, the combination of industrial, commercial, agricultural, and financial interests in one person or family group, and the frequent absence of reliable data on the business population had to be taken into account. To avoid possible bias in the distribution of attitudes due to excessive concentration on one type of business, the interviews were aimed at a cross section of managers from a great variety of industrial, commercial, and financial enterprises. A conscious and largely successful effort was also made to interview certain top representatives of leading business families, without whose presence any managerial sample in the countries included would have been incomplete.

The great majority of interviewees were natives of the country concerned. Because of the importance of the foreign-born element in Latin American management, however, the sample included a number of foreign-born persons with real roots in their adopted country.

Although most of the companies had 100 or more employees, medium-sized firms were also represented. Very small businesses were included only in a few cases where it seemed important to ascertain the views of owner-managers. The industries or business activities represented include textiles, clothing, shoes, food processing, lumber, ceramics, chemicals, metal products, electrical equipment, mining, construction, commerce, banking, and insurance.

All the interviews were conducted by the author, who explained the academic nature of the study and the confidential character of the interview. Refusals of interviews were extremely rare, though in some cases the potential interviewee was out of the country or could not be reached in the time available. Some interviewees had more to say than others, but in general cooperation was very much the rule. An attempt was made to carry out every interview with only the two principals present, but in some cases the interviewee called in other members of the executive staff in order to help him supply all the information required, or for other reasons of his own. In some cases he considered the interview a fairly important and interesting event to be shared with his colleagues, and although their attendance may have somewhat affected the interview situation, the net result was probably more detailed answers than would have been obtained otherwise.

Contradictions between answers were not infrequent, but conscious misrepresentation to interviewers is probably far less frequent than many laymen believe. In an appropriate interview setting, the interviewee feels intellectually challenged and stimulated to such an extent that he talks frankly and openly. Rationalizations, of course, are no less common in enterprise managers than in other people and it is part of the researcher's assignment to perceive them. In this case, however, most interviewees seemed to feel—rightly or wrongly—that a foreign economist with academic background and interests would be more detached and trustworthy than an interviewer of the manager's own national background. The interview was thus welcomed as a rare opportunity to speak out. There was very little evidence of interviewees telling the interviewer what they thought he would like to hear, an occurrence that otherwise is not infrequent in cultures characterized by politeness.

The managerial terminology fluctuates not only from one country to another but often within the same country. *Gerente, director, presidente, administrador, superintendente, socio, director-gerente,* and *presidente-gerente* were some of the titles encountered, but in some cases there seemed to be no definite title at all. In any event, the interviews were held in the great majority of cases with the top manager of the company concerned, regardless of whether he was owner, partner, or hired executive. In a few cases the interviewee was vice-president, plant director, or sales manager.

A terminological question also exists concerning the use of the words "enterprise," "business," "administration," "manager," and "executive." For the purpose of this study, *enterprise* is a broader concept than *business*. Although the sample consisted mainly of the heads of private enterprises it also included a number of managers of publicly owned enterprises. Actually one of the latter, in Northeast Brazil, was also a *fazendeiro* (rural estate owner) in private life. We shall use the word *manager* to characterize the head of a private or public enterprise, *executive* to describe either the leading or a lesser figure in management, *businessman* to denote the head or owner of one or more private enterprises, *administrator* to describe a hired manager of a private or public enterprise, and *entrepreneur* to characterize anyone involved in innovating risk-taking initiative.

The book is organized as follows:

The first chapter offers an outline of the general social setting of management in Latin America, chiefly for the reader who has no specialized knowledge of that area. It discusses such factors as the agrarian basis of the economy, the Indian heritage, and the relationship between family status, business, and politics.

The next six chapters are based more directly on the interview materials of the study and are designed to show how Latin American enterprise managers interpret important aspects of national economic development and their own role in it.

Chapter II is concerned with special characteristics of population as perceived by the enterprise managers of each country. Clearly the managers' view of favorable or unfavorable traits of the population will color their judgment of the prospects and needs of economic development.

• Chapter III discusses the managers' interpretation of their own background as a group, and describes the selection, promotion, and training needs of executive personnel, including foreign participation in such training, as viewed by the managers themselves.

• Chapter IV takes up more broadly the ways in which Latin American managers perceive their own aims and activity in relation to the economic development needs of their nation, the respective roles of profit and nonprofit factors in managerial decisions, and the sources of managerial satisfactions and dissatisfactions.

More specific aspects of the self-perception of the managers as a functional economic group—namely, their interpretations of competition, investment and capital supply, risk, and productivity—are discussed in Chapter V.

Whereas Chapters III, IV, and V deal with the managers' view of various aspects of their own activity and their role in the process of economic development, Chapter VI discusses their perception of the role of the government in economic development, especially in education, agrarian reform, industrialization, and financial policy, and also treats the views encountered regarding the relationship between inflation and development.

This discussion of the perceived private and public contribution to economic development is followed up in Chapter VII by an account of managerial views in Latin America concerning the foreign role in the national development process. The beliefs of managers in respect to the past record and future possibilities of foreign investment in their country, to foreign aid (including the Alliance for Progress), and to Latin American economic integration are described.

Chapters VIII and IX discuss the significance of all these findings for the development process in Latin America, including the impact on management of cultural and institutional variations among the countries of this area, the extent of entrepreneurial initiative in Latin America, the possibilities for an incorporation of managerial activity into development planning, and certain policy implications both for the Latin American governments and for the United States.

ENTERPRISE *in* LATIN AMERICA
Business Attitudes in a Developing Economy

1

The Social Setting of
Management in Latin America

BEFORE the results of the interview study are presented in detail, a brief discussion in general terms of the social, economic, and political setting of enterprise management in Latin America may be helpful to the reader.

Agrarian basis. In most of the countries in this region, a large sector of business—not only sugar refineries, canning plants, and textile mills but also transportation enterprises, commerce, and banking—is based directly or indirectly on agriculture. The degree of dependence varies from country to country, being smaller, for example, in Chile with its rather diversified industry and mining, and greater in Guatemala and Uruguay. This dependence is also influenced by the historical prevalence of monoculture, predominant cultivation of one crop—coffee, sugar, or bananas —though the tendency has been weakening in recent years.

This strong agricultural basis of business is colored by the feudal legacy of Latin America. Here again there are great and sometimes paradoxical differences among nations. Bolivia, the poorest country in South America, carried out a far-reaching land reform after the revolution of 1952. Although some of the expectations connected with it have not yet been fulfilled, feudal traditions have rapidly been coming to an end, and the Indian peasant has been increasingly integrated into the nation.

On the other hand, Chile, which in general is an economically and politically more advanced country, is only now beginning to change its system of *fundos*—privately owned rural estates of sometimes enormous size. Sizable numbers of *inquilinos*, or farm laborers—who often spend their entire lives working on a large estate and who depend on its owner economically and socially—are now learning to read and write, and perhaps send some of their children to the city, but the *inquilino* is still a not-too-distant relative of the feudal serf. The owner of the *fundo*, it is true, may also be active in urban business and may have an office and house in the city. The international movement toward land reform has thus reached the various countries of South America in an extremely uneven degree.

The Indian heritage. Important differences in enterprise settings also exist between the "Indian" and "non-Indian" areas. The connotation of the term "Indian" in this region is not primarily racial or ethnic. The foreign visitor may at first be surprised to hear people who to *him* look like pure-bred Indians refer to *los Indios* as if they were inferior beings from another planet. It is not uncommon to hear the claim made by Chileans that there are no Indians in Chile, sometimes accompanied by the explanation that the Arau-canos never surrendered and were all killed by the Span-iards. Yet Indian ethnic types are quite common in Chile too, especially among the poorer classes.

The real explanation is that the term "Indian" has largely a socioeconomic and cultural rather than purely ethnic connotation in Latin America. Indians are not simply peo-ple who "look like Indians" but people who live in rural communities of a more or less tribal type, though they now increasingly veer toward the fringes of cities; who employ ancient methods of land cultivation that yield barely enough food to feed themselves even in "good" years; peo-ple who lack ambition, drive, or hope of improving their economic condition through better or less wasteful use of land; people who have hardly any time perspective in their economic behavior and rarely perceive a need for saving or storing goods against a future contingency.

The Indians in this sense live outside the national mar-kets. They sell and buy next to nothing, with the sole ex-ception of a local village market where some fruits, vegetables, pottery, or baskets may be traded, chiefly among themselves. Any concept of "business" or "manage-ment" in the European, North American, or even Latin American urban sense is inapplicable to the Indians as a socioeconomic and cultural group. Their language is some Indian dialect; whether they also speak Spanish depends on how much schooling, if any, they have had. Their propor-tion of the total population varies greatly, from a majority in Guatemala, Bolivia, Peru, and Ecuador to a minority in Colombia and Mexico. They are almost wholly absent in Chile and Uruguay.

Some of the countries mentioned have often been characterized as having a "dual economy." Of the 11 million Peruvians, for instance, only 3 or 4 million are considered to be part of the national market, while the others live their own economic life quite apart from the general business processes. The concept of dual economy contains a substantial element of truth but does not tell the full story of very complex relationships. There is constant financial pressure on the government to spend money on the nonintegrated sector of the national economy for roads, schools, police, or public health, and those financial needs are often seen by business as an economically sterile burden. Traditionally few enterprise managers have thought of the Indians as a great potential market or have oriented managerial decisions in any such direction. There is also a good deal of fear toward the Indians once they "wake up" and perhaps become the easy prey of demagogues, and a good many businessmen and others would prefer to leave them in their dormant state even though it keeps them out of the national market.

Family status, business, and politics. The cultural setting of enterprise in Latin America shows a combination of Indian and Iberian influences with some admixture of Western European, North American, or African elements. The resulting atmosphere is characterized by strong needs for high social status. These needs reflect partly the strict, though different, social hierarchies both in Iberian and Indian societies, and the additional desire of businessmen to be clearly differentiated from the low-status, sometimes Indian or Negro groups in their society. The personality forma-

O

The Social Setting of Management

tion of the upper- or middle-class child is usually dominated by such status factors or needs of his family. If he becomes a businessman or enterprise manager, he will continue to be dominated by such influences in his entire way of life, including daily decisions in the company.

This means that he tends to consider business not as an impersonal activity of "economic man" directed at maximization of profit but as an extension of his family's drive for social status. The family supplies his financial contacts, perhaps his initial job, and the links to influential politicians and bureaucrats without which it is impossible to get business transactions done. In a small economy where "everybody knows everybody" and where taxes, import permits, licenses, and government orders often depend on personal contacts and political pull—even when there is no corruption in a crude sense—the social standing of the businessman and his family are of decisive importance.

For related reasons there is widespread lack of specialization in a definite industry or field of business (discussed in the next two sections). The same person, family group, or office frequently administers a variety of enterprises which may range from textile plants and sugar plantations to mines and banks. It is often felt that in the existing economic structure businessmen cannot afford to specialize.[1]

The interconnection of business and management with family relationships and politics will be discussed in some detail in Chapter III. Managers are frequently selected on the basis of family links and class origin, rather than special-

[1] See *Management of Industrial Enterprises in Underdeveloped Countries* (New York: United Nations, 1958), pp. 4ff. Also Professor Cochran's findings on cultural factors in Puerto Rican business: Thomas C. Cochran, *The Puerto Rican Businessman: A Study in Cultural Change* (Philadelphia: University of Pennsylvania Press, 1959), Chap. IV.

ized training. They constantly use political pull in order to get things done or to secure special favors for their companies. A company manager may also put in a short period of service as public administrator or cabinet minister without necessarily discontinuing his interests in private enterprise. Class barriers to successful business activity account in part for the widespread quest for government positions. Money made through the political medium may then go into new or old enterprises and the *político* may transform himself into an entrepreneur.[2] In their basic mentality concerning the conduct of business, national development needs, and life values in general, managers in Latin America thus tend to differ greatly at this point from their colleagues in more developed parts of the world.

Enterprise structure. Considerable strength of family links continues to prevail not only in the ownership but in the management of companies in most parts of Latin America. Although a number of firms with widely dispersed stock ownership exist in such areas as Mexico City and São Paulo, and though their managers like to express their pride in such wide distribution, this type of ownership is still the exception rather than the rule.

The legal form of *sociedad anónima* is frequently chosen now but the actual ownership of the shares typically remains in the hands of a small or large family group, perhaps with the participation of some close friends of the family. Such family-centered ownership, it is true, is often con-

[2] Compare the typology of managerial élites, including patrimonial, political, and professional management, as presented by Frederick F. Harbison and Charles A. Myers, *Management in the Industrial World* (New York: McGraw-Hill, 1959), Chap. 4. Also Fritz Redlich, "Business Leadership: Diverse Origins and Variant Forms," *Economic Development and Cultural Change*, Vol. VI, No. 3 (April, 1958).

fined to the majority or a sizable minority of the shares. In recent years, trends to wider distribution of shares, or at least ambitions in this direction, have emerged in an increasing number of areas. There are complaints, though, that new equity investors tend to expect a fixed "rent" and various guarantees.

In some cases a family-owned enterprise employs hired high-level executives from outside the family, but more frequently family influence extends not only to ownership but to management. In other words, the managerial group in a given firm is likely to come entirely or in large part from the family, though some of the relatives concerned—especially the young ones—may also have received executive training. The managers usually consider this an appropriate arrangement under the conditions of their country or have not even thought of alternatives.

As is shown in Chapter III, there is increasing emphasis on the need for systematic executive training of some kind. The present trend can, therefore, best be described as favoring the family-rooted manager who has acquired sound professional background. In a few cases, such as an architects' firm in Mexico, a more directly professional association (in this case of former university colleagues) was found to be present in the ownership structure of a company.

Lack of specialization. We have mentioned already the frequent combination of disparate firms within one, usually family-rooted, interest group. This, of course, is different from building up a multitude of *related* firms for tax reasons. The same individuals or family might hold a dominating interest in a coffee plantation, textile mill, construction firm, export business, and bank, for example. In most cases no economic link exists between the activities of these

firms other than the fact that they are owned or controlled
by the same people and share their financial resources, and
that they are all concretely or vaguely expected to be
profitable. In wide areas managers consider such a combination the most suitable arrangement for successful business operations—perhaps the only possible one. The
following comment from an industrialist interviewed in
El Salvador is worth noting:

The industrial part of our interests is growing constantly. The
agrarian part is "incidental"; the commercial comes from the
industrial, and the financial comes from the others. Coffee, of
course, has been the *matriz*. There has been economic intui-
tion in our expansion but no economic system. The entire enterprise has traditionally been based on the family, but with the
transition from one form of enterprise to others the inclusion of
people and capital from other sources has become necessary.
However, we have always had the initiative. There has been
a definite logic in our industrial and other interests. People have
sought us out as a catalyst; we share our experience with others.
This could serve as pattern in other countries, but it should not
be done with so few people. The young ones should have more
training in economics, government and sociology.

The activity and mentality of many managers have been
shaped decisively by such arrangements. Instead of concentrating on the efficient management of a company within
his own field of professional training, an executive has to
switch his attention continuously from, say, production
problems in a textile factory to the sale of coffee abroad or
to the credit decisions of a bank. His prime loyalty is to the
real boss, the top man of the entire combination of interests,
not to any individual firm. In fact, without the top man's
political links and family standing little could be achieved in
the conduct of *any* of these firms, and informal conversa-

tions with friends or influential people take up a very substantial part of the top man's activity. Since the latter thus occupies a unique and authoritarian position, delegation of his major activities is considered impossible by himself and the others.

The explanation for this pattern of acting and thinking is, of course, largely to be found in historical factors. As mentioned earlier, most enterprises had their roots in agricultural holdings which, under a suitable stimulus or market threat, were expanded into processing, commerce, banking, and eventually nonrelated industrial activities. This process, not to be confounded with systematic diversification, still continues in large parts of Latin America and partly explains the limitations of business specialization.

To this must be added the traditional scarcity of clearcut industrial opportunities and the frequent urge to invest inflationary gains in some form of enterprise or other. Eventually the ownership of industries and banks also comes to confer prestige upon an originally agrarian family. At any rate, the historical explanation does not alter the fact that the executive's thinking is shaped in large part by the constant pressure to be on the alert for new fields of business expansion and to solve problems which arise from the lack of integration or industrial logic within the varied and shifting holdings of the top man and his family group.

The pattern described should not, however, be interpreted as the only one in existence. There are some examples of genuine upstream integration, for example, in the tobacco business in Northeast Brazil. There is also a multitude of more or less independent small enterprises some of which have been established precisely to get away from family pressures. At the other extreme, there are a few corporations in the North American sense of the word with several thousands of stockholders each. It cannot be assumed that the enterprise pattern in Latin America is necessarily headed toward the kind of corporation that exists in the United States or Germany. Still, the trend appears to be toward greater specialization in the ownership and, especially, in the management of enterprises, and toward fuller and more expert use of capital resources than has existed traditionally.

The short-range view. In most of the areas concerned, business is still characterized by orientation toward immediate results, mostly to the neglect of long-range considerations. Often the very perception of long-range goals is missing. This does not necessarily mean that investment cannot be intended to keep yielding profits for years; but the cases are still fairly rare in which an investment is even considered unless it promises to start yielding high profits immediately and to amortize itself completely within a very few years.

The reasons given by businessmen and managers for this prevalence of the short-run approach vary greatly, as will be shown later in greater detail. Some will remark smilingly that people in general just behave in this fashion in their country. Others blame this particular approach on the perennial instability of governments and political forces, which makes any long-range business planning impossible. Still others point out that the shortage of capital and credit facilities, and the resulting level of interest rates, are such that no enterprise could afford to wait for years until its investments begin to yield substantial profits.

Finally, many of these countries have had recent experiences with inflation or live under the constant threat of it, and any long-run view is considered impracticable in an inflationary atmosphere. In Chile, inflationary experiences are now some 85 years old, with various fluctuations and a more acute phase during the 1950s so that there are now several generations of people who have never lived in a noninflationary society. Even so, one is more likely to encounter examples of the longer view in some countries than in others. This distinction indicates that the differential factors mentioned earlier—including the cultural and political setting—must be of considerable influence.

Casual work habits. The concurrence of certain cultural and status factors explains in large part the paradoxical fact that the short-range mentality has not brought with it a general spirit of profit maximization. Mostly there is a drive for immediate high profits, especially when they require little effort, but no attempt to maximize them through systematic decision-making and performance. The political and family contacts described require a casual, easygoing way of doing business. One cannot afford to make an influential man nervous by annoying him too frequently in the interest of monetary business opportunities; it "just isn't done," and may backfire if attempted. Moreover, the cultural traditions both of the Iberians and the Indians, and in some areas the climate as well, counteract any relentless, "rational" drive toward constant maximization of profit. The time-honored concentration of economic interests on consumption—especially on luxury consumption in the upper classes—rather than on production and service, also remains a retarding factor in many parts of Latin America.

Where leisure, contemplation, or merely an unhurried way of going about things and avoidance of worry about the future represent predominant values in life, regular split-second decisions or rigid datelines, even for loan payments, may be at odds with cultural assumptions. In fact, they may even be incompatible with the personal touch and the informal utilization of political or family contacts which have traditionally been essential in the conduct of business in these countries.

Work habits of management *and* labor, therefore, are different from those in North America or Western Europe. Visitors from these parts of the world are inclined to conclude that Latin Americans are just "lazy," but what is really involved is a different way of looking at life in general and at economic activities in particular. Not to be rushed is for many a basic principle of life; what good is a little more profit or pay if it involves continuous hurry? This does not mean, of course, that financial incentives are ineffective; very often they have much effect. But this is the case only when they are strong enough to overcome that basic attitude, and if they are also connected with personal involvement in the job to be done. Otherwise, a one-day fiesta such as July 28 in Peru, August 6 in Bolivia, or September 18 in Chile, will become the pretext to take things easy for a week or two. This, we repeat, is no less true of management than of labor. The whole idea of high production and a rising level of productivity being the basis of economic welfare is still rather new and in some quarters completely unknown, though it is considerably more widespread in some areas than in others. On the whole, management is still conducted in a work atmosphere which does not lend itself quite easily to a systematic drive for constant improvement and expansion of business.

Foreign influence in management. In all the countries under discussion, the quantitative and qualitative share of foreigners in management has been substantial. This is true far beyond those companies which are largely or entirely foreign-owned. The latter, in fact, tend increasingly to hire or train native executives who are to collaborate with "imported" ones and to help in avoiding a public impression that foreign elements are taking over the country's economy. But "native" enterprises are quite often managed by immigrants or their sons, who have found it relatively easy to advance in countries where there has long been a shortage of trained executives. The first- or second-generation executives are mostly of European but sometimes of Arab or North American origin, and are usually closer to the managerial standards of more developed countries than are their old-stock confrères whose business concepts they often find exasperating.

To this comes the important role of foreign capital, and the ambivalent interpretation given to it by domestic business (discussed in Chapter VII) and, to some extent, by the general population. Foreign capital has been instrumental in the development of mining (copper, nitrates, tin, and oil, in particular, depending on the country), of transportation and commerce, and, to a lesser extent, of agricultural plantations and processing (cotton, sugar, coffee). There is also important foreign investment in industry, both light and heavy. The role of foreign executives varies greatly. Certain foreign-owned companies, especially those that have been there for a long time, employ many native executives, including some in higher positions, while others rely chiefly on an imported executive staff.

Social radicalism. In all of Latin America, business is conducted in a more or less strong atmosphere of social radicalism that dominates a substantial sector of society. This sentiment is often centered in labor unions and in the universities, although agrarian elements have also played an important part in it, as in Bolivia. Such social radicalism has usually had its roots in a long history of unfulfilled claims of workers and peasants against socially irresponsible managers, landowners, and governments. These claims have involved, in particular, livable wages, social insurance, protection against loan sharks and corrupt bureaucrats, just taxation, and land reform. But this historical justification of radical reform programs does not alter the fact that they are sometimes misinterpreted in our period in a way that betrays economic ignorance or demagoguery. The complexion of social radicalism has ranged from the mild if vague reformism of the APRA in Peru to outright communism, but in each country private management is carried out under the shadow of radical threats to which it often reacts with equal intransigence. The feeling that fundamental socioeconomic changes are unavoidable and that they should not be left to the drastic methods of *fidelismo* has increasingly influenced the atmosphere of business and management but is by no means universal yet.

Radical movements, to be sure, are not to be confounded with the strong economic role which the *government* occupies in these countries almost regardless of its ideological complexion. This role ranges from military budgets and the construction of roads and schools to direct investment in power plants, oil wells, or steel enterprises, particularly where the supply of private capital is scarce. Business opinion mostly approves of the former types of government activity, but is at least divided when the latter type—that is, direct government investment and, especially, government management in industry, commerce, or finance—is concerned. In any case, private management is continually faced both with the help and with the competition and complication that are presented by widespread government activities in the economic field.

The cultural, institutional, and attitudinal setting of enterprise management in Latin America is thus characterized by a number of influences which are peculiar to that region, in addition to some other influences more nearly related to those underlying managerial activities in North America and Western Europe.

Only a minority of enterprise managers in contemporary Latin America can be characterized as entrepreneurs either in an individual or a collective sense, a point which is discussed more fully in Chapter VIII. The legacy of Iberian feudalism and, in many parts, of Indian cultures is still psychologically strong even where it has been substantially weakened or abolished in its institutional sense. The expectation of public intervention in business through various kinds of aid ranging from education to investment funds and tariff protection remains high. At the same time, political restrictions and social radicalism keep causing uneasiness among enterprise managers.

The interaction between family status, management, and politics is taken for granted, and managerial decisions are often colored by status needs of the family. Paternalist attitudes toward the workers and within the executive group have been gradually weakening but are still considerable. Professionally trained management and objective criteria of executive selection and promotion are a rather new and not yet widespread phenomenon. Specialization of enterprises and managers has been impeded by the family basis of business and the smallness of markets which is often considered permanent. Short-range thinking still prevails but is rarely coupled with systematic maximization of profits.

To these factors must be added intensive managerial perceptions of specific characteristics of the population in each country, and sometimes in Latin America as a whole, perceptions which color the managers' general interpretation of the environment in which their decisions and actions take place. This influence will be discussed in Chapter II on the basis of interview data.

The more general purpose of the interview study whose results will be reported in the following chapters was not, of course, to collect material for criticism of Latin American enterprise management from a Western, "superior" point of view but to help students of economic development understand the institutional and attitudinal problems which managers are faced with in one newly developing area of international interest.

II

Perceived Characteristics
of the Population

THE way in which enterprise management functions in a
newly developing area depends in a large degree on the
way in which it relates itself to the general population. This
relationship was considered likely to affect the views of
Latin American managers concerning executive selection,
productivity, competition, the role of government, and
other specific aspects of the development process which
will be discussed in later chapters.

An item in the questionnaire consequently attempted to
find out whether enterprise managers in each country felt

that its people showed special characteristics that affected the conduct of business and the course of economic development, or whether the managers perceived development needs in more general terms without national or cultural distinctions.[1]

Most interviewees were strongly interested in this question and stimulated by it. Only a few thought that their countrymen showed no special traits at all compared with other Latin Americans, Europeans, or North Americans. Those who answered in this vein mostly felt that business and underdevelopment presented the same problems everywhere, that human nature was the same throughout the world, or that education was more important than nationality.

Latin American Traits

Among the majority who answered affirmatively, it is true, a substantial number commented in terms of Latin American, rather than national, traits. In other words, when asked whether the Salvadoreño, for instance, showed any special characteristics, some interviewees in El Salvador replied that he did but that they were essentially the same as those of other Latinos, a claim which was then usually followed by enumeration of such traits.

This might have been a justifiable answer if the respondents had been thoroughly familiar with Latin America, but most of them definitely were not. The number of those who had been to Europe or the United States but had never visited at length any other Latin American country was quite considerable in each country covered. The mutual knowledge of Brazilians, especially those from the

[1] "Do you think that people in this country show any special traits which affect business and development or not?"

isolated Northeast, and Spanish-Americans seemed particularly limited.

In other words, many interviewees assumed without any empirical evidence at their disposal that other Latin Americans were just like the people of their own country, and then answered the question in terms of important differences between Latin Americans on the one hand and Europeans, North Americans, and everyone else on the other. Comments on basic differences between the people of the United States and those of Latin America were especially frequent and sometimes referred to the inability of North American visitors, experts, or politicians to understand that this was *not* just like the United States only less so.

Customs are different here from Europe. The cultural stages differ, especially the consciousness of productivity. We need a change in the concept of *empresario*, in the mentality. We need a Christian spirit of justice. (Industrial manager, Mexico.)

In this case the question about special traits of the population had elicited a response in normative terms—the traits which it *should* have.

Among those who listed special characteristics either of their own people or of Latin Americans in general, some emphasized favorable traits while a somewhat smaller group concentrated on perceived adverse characteristics. Good traits along with bad were also listed by a substantial number.

Brazilians are the most soft-hearted people in the world, and extremism would be impossible here. They may be strict for a moment but will then do whatever you want. They are easygoing, like to do favors, but are disorganized. Here in Bahia we have the best people in the country; they are cooperative toward others (though not commercially). But greater local pride would have dynamic effects. There is no real "local patriotism" here as in São Paulo or Minas Gerais. (Industrial manager, Bahia, Northeast Brazil.)

In another area of Northeast Brazil, a sugar producer characterized his rural workers as intelligent but undisciplined, "consumed by their poverty" and lacking in stimuli for improvement. It was also said repeatedly that the North-easterner had suffered more and thereby had become tougher than other Brazilians.

Somewhat different responses were encountered in Mexico:

Comparisons are difficult, but Mexicans show indifference, patience, irresponsibility, and boldness. There is constant progress, though. (Lawyer and businessman, Mexico.)

A foreign commercial manager in Mexico claimed that Mexicans have no loyalty toward a company or group, merely toward a leader; not only did they follow Villa and Zapata but the salesmen follow their sales manager when he moves to another company. Another national trait, in his view, is an artificial, demagogic nationalism with defensive attitudes toward "imperialism" and foreign goods. But an industrialist in another area of the same country felt that Mexicans are, above all, influenced by religious factors, think less than others of money as an aim of life, tend to belong rigidly to political groupings, but are also individualistic and have difficulty in accepting *factores socializantes*.

In Guatemala, the managers interviewed tended to draw favorable comparisons in terms of honesty or working capacity between their own people and other Latin Americans, but it was also pointed out that land and food were relatively plentiful compared with some other Latin countries and there was therefore less external pressure for hard work. One Guatemalan interviewee characterized his countryman as astute, though he hides it; he is not especially brave but not a coward; is curious but opposed to ostentation; *simpático* but not very enterprising, and fond of the exotic and romantic.

Favorable Traits

Among the favorable traits that were most frequently mentioned everywhere, intelligence and learning ability stood out. All the way from Mexico and Guatemala to Chile and Brazil managers appeared to have predominantly a high opinion about the innate ability of workers in their nation to "catch on" to somewhat complicated mechanical processes if properly instructed. Likewise most managers considered the people of their respective countries, including their own workers, normally helpful and cooperative whenever radical agitators were absent. In El Salvador and Northeast Brazil, especially Ceará, there was also repeated praise of the persistent hard work and ingenuity of which the common people there were considered to be well capable when stimulated in appropriate ways. In Mexico, an industrial manager of European origin claimed that Mexicans are the most *stable* of Latin Americans and that they have a good sense of humor. Another one pointed out that the Mexican businessman is used to much courtesy and diplomacy, in contrast to the North American, though the latter sometimes learns it eventually and finds out that "business is *not* business."

In Venezuela, many interviewees felt that the far-reaching mixture of races there had resulted in greater opportunity for everybody and less tradition-bound class prejudice than in most other Latin American countries.

Many a Venezuelan grows up in a semimatriarchal family and knows no authority or emotive formation. He is very equalitarian, thinks he is equal to any sage or pasha. (Manager, financial company, Venezuela.)

The Venezuelan still confounds freedom to dissent with freedom of conspiring to overthrow his opponents. He is still immature, but is also equalitarian. (Industrial manager, Venezuela.)

Adverse Traits

On the other hand, adverse comments were expressed in a substantial number of cases and areas. Some of these comments were made in terms of generalization about people in tropical areas, but most referred to the local population or to Latin Americans in general. The number-one complaint may be summed up in the word *apathy*. A good many managers felt that the combination of Indian, Iberian, and feudal influences had resulted in characteristics variously described as laziness, indifference, lack of ambition, lack of understanding for teamwork, timidity in doing business, dependence on the state, inability to look beyond the necessities of the moment and to plan ahead, even violence and destructiveness. Lack of reliability or punctuality, and individualistic righteousness were also mentioned. So were lack of forthrightness, the habit of "fixing" things instead of paying taxes, for instance, and unnecessary feelings of inferiority toward foreigners.

Many such statements probably expressed the prevailing stereotypes of upper social groups about the lower, but the mere existence of such perceptions is an important fact. A Brazilian manager claimed that in the relations among executives and between the latter and their workers, Brazilians are far more informal than Europeans, more like North

Americans; but also that Brazilians originated in "three sad populations" and have much (sometimes too much) human sympathy and tolerance. A foreign-born businessman in El Salvador commented:

The upper class here suffers from lack of *cultura*. Dependence on one product has affected their morality and behavior in *good* years; they have no ambition, no drive for better living. The climate also has a similar influence. Only the small middle group, to the extent that it exists in this mostly agricultural society, really wants progress actively. There is a basic long-range problem of education.

External Influences

Adverse judgments about the population in general were often related to ideas about external factors which, it was thought, had caused such traits to develop or survive. The most frequent of these qualifications referred either to lack of physical and mental stamina due to malnutrition, with resulting limitations to work efficiency, or to lack of education with a resulting prevalence of irrational reactions. Many of those who criticized the lack of ambition, foresight, staying power, or sense of obligations—not only of rights—in their workers or in the general population added that these shortcomings were being, or could be, overcome by better educational facilities for the common man. Some, it is true, considered the latter hopeless, and among these pessimists racial beliefs were influential. On the other hand, the racial mixture concerned was regarded by others as a favorable factor in combining the religious background, native intelligence, and physical sturdiness of the European, Indian, and African elements.

There are two groups in Latin America. Mexico is part of the "Indian" group, that's the main difference. I have nothing against the Indians. This is *not* a race problem but one of education and living standards. In Mexico we have found the best solution yet. (Industrial manager, Mexico.)

The Mexican worker has an enormous capacity for adaptation but he is irresponsible. After the annual revision of contracts, productivity diminishes for two or three months, then it goes up again. (Lawyer and businessman, Mexico.)

Those responses which were on the favorable or optimistic side often revealed a good deal of national pride and a sense of uniqueness of the favorable traits concerned. In Northeast Brazil, it was claimed repeatedly that the people of this region, or of the state concerned, even though poorer are more authentic Brazilians than those of the South with its many recent immigrants. Interestingly, this was even said by some foreign-born managers. An industrial promoter in Mexico characterized his countrymen as democratic, individualistic, proud, independent, and Christian. There was little indication anywhere of nationalism in an aggressive sense or in that of a *Herrenvolk* chosen for leadership by nature. There was, however, a widespread feeling that not only the conduct of company management but the national development policy needed to take the special traits of the people into account and to avoid any blind application of methods derived from peoples with a different culture and mentality. Statements to this effect, it is true, were sometimes accompanied by rationalizations about the causes of past or present delays in economic and social progress.

Some responses to this question were given in terms of institutional or historical factors. According to an industrialist in El Salvador, the fact that this is the most densely populated country on the continent had led the people to realize that they had to work hard in order to survive. An industrial manager in Mexico pointed out that corporate enterprises in his country are quite different from those in the United States; they are not publicity-minded but secretive and "closed" regardless of whether their condition is good or bad, and the fear of taxes makes them desire to appear as poor as possible.

National habits of cutthroat competition and political pull were mentioned in various countries. So were the rural characteristics and limited consumption habits of the majority of the population. In Venezuela rising quality standards of consumers and installment buying were thought by some to be attributable to the long history of importation from the United States based largely on oil revenues. However, the frequency of wasteful consumption and spending by people who had never had savings was also pointed out. An Argentinian living in Chile claimed that the Chilean is the born consumer who keeps buying even when prices go up whereas Argentinians react quite differently. He saw the Chileans as more *simpáticos* but also more introvert than his countrymen. A Cuban-born executive in Venezuela commented:

People are very intelligent here but have had little luck in having their minds improved. In Cuba, everybody wanted to learn and improve; here, there are many poor people without ambitions or horizons. Moreover, there is no real middle class, only foreigners. In 150 years of "freedom" there have been only dictators. They don't know any other conditions. People like me here because I am used to democratic ways.

A public-enterprise executive in the same country saw the main characteristics of its people in heavy reliance on living off the oil-rich government.

In summary, enterprise managers were greatly interested in the question about special characteristics of their people, and mostly related some such characteristics to the general setting in which their managerial activity took place. Rarely was enterprise management thought of as an abstract technique that was applicable, without much change, in any part of the world. Specific responses to the question concerned ranged from general statements on the ways in which human nature manifests itself in their country to emphasis on either favorable or adverse characteristics of their own people which required careful consideration in the interest both of effective enterprise management and of national development policy. Depending on the country, the "favorable characteristics" listed included astuteness, ability to learn and to work hard, generosity modified by individualism, and pride in one's heritage. The "adverse traits" included disorganization, lack of discipline or reliability, inability to plan ahead, and apathy.

In the chapters that follow we shall discuss concrete applications of these beliefs to personnel policy, competition, investment, politics, and other aspects of economic development.

III

Executive Selection and Training

HOW do Latin American managers view their own background and function in comparison with the characteristics of the population in general? In particular, what do they feel is the most appropriate way to select executive personnel and what are the criteria of executive promotion? This was the subject of one of the questions asked.[1]

Selection and Promotion of Executives

Not unexpectedly, the question turned out to be inapplicable to a number of companies whose executive personnel

[1] "What are the criteria of this company in selecting and promoting executive personnel?"

was either identical with the owners or consisted entirely of their relatives. In an enterprise owned and run by several brothers, for instance, the answer is obvious. Likewise, in a firm where the general manager originally got into the company and subsequently was promoted to the top position because he was the nephew of the founder, no such question need be asked.[2] It was found, however, that for business purposes a family group could be quite large, and that in some family enterprises the executive staff was bolstered by trained executives from outside the family. In various companies there was a definite feeling that further expansion would necessitate a search for executive talent, as well as capital, from outside sources.

Every company needs an appropriate executive structure. We make people rise within the organization whenever possible; this gives better results. The qualities required are absolute honesty, a sense of responsibility, desire for progress, ability to adapt and to get along with people, and "punch." Technical knowledge *we* can teach them. Our father taught my brothers and me about this business since we were three years old. Later he made each of us specialize. (Industrial manager, Mexico.)

In those cases where the answer was not implicit in the family structure of the enterprise, the prevailing response was that the company promotes people from within when-

---

[2] "In the Latin American culture, business is a part of the total scheme of things: It is part of the family, of the *compadre* relation, of friendships, and of the Church. Business is done among friends in a leisurely and understanding way. Material success is at the bottom of the scale. First of all comes the protection of the family, the *compadres,* the friends," Frank Tannenbaum, *Ten Keys to Latin America* (New York: Columbia University Press, 1963), p. 129. Compare Frank Brandenburg, *The Development of Latin American Private Enterprise* (Washington: National Planning Association, 1964).

ever possible and looks for outside sources of executive personnel only when it cannot help it. Some respondents were almost dogmatic about it and mostly explained their attitude by the need to have people who shared their way of thinking.

There is no pool of executives in this country. We have to depend on our own people and to train them gradually even *after* they have been given some nice title such as sales manager or production chief. There is no use in special courses, which are very bad here. We start with *ingenieros* or *abogados* who have executive ability and financial understanding. (Vice-president, mining company, Mexico.)

Considerations of seniority were not mentioned as such, but there was occasional association of long experience with efficient performance and, thereby, executive promotion. The manager of a partly foreign-owned firm in Mexico stressed their desire to employ Mexican executives, or at least people who have the feel of the country and identify with it. Similar statements were also made in comparable cases in various other countries.

In the least developed areas, however, the statement was frequently made that companies could not afford to be choosy since the few good executives available tended to start enterprises of their own. The shortage of executive personnel in Northeast Brazil, for instance, and the superior competition of São Paulo and Rio de Janeiro were often seen as reducing the choice to one person at best as there were no others from whom to choose. But even in one of the most rapidly growing areas of Mexico, an industrialist commented:

In this country there is a great problem in getting competent persons. There are no professional managers yet for whom management is a vocation. We have to observe executives at work, to see whether they are completely responsible on the job and whether they are creative and expansive. Personal traits such as "ideology," honesty, and sanity are very much taken into account, but we cannot afford to be "scientific" about it.

And a financial manager in Chile when reinterviewed in 1963 claimed that there still was difficulty in getting a good *medium* executive who could rise above the department-head level even though *top* managers were available in Chile for a variety of enterprises unless they required special knowledge in a new field.

In those areas where the shortage of executive personnel was not viewed as being too severe, *personal* traits were often mentioned along with educational and technical background and production-mindedness as being equally or more important. It was pointed out in various ways that technical competence can be taught but character, enthusiasm, and loyalty cannot. In other cases the yardstick of selection and promotion was viewed as depending primarily on the nature of the job. Executives whose assignments involve extensive contact with people (such as sales managers or industrial-relations experts) were usually thought of as requiring definite personal traits such as "getting along with people" or being able to decide and command, while supervision of machines was not associated with such traits.

Some people have a flair for management. The best manager is the one who can pick a really good team. This is the secret of this company. Delegation of management is equally important and he should be able to learn it. One should never be afraid to teach others either. The manager should get along with others as friends, not have his foot at the others' necks. There has been a rush of "courses" on management and it's a good thing, but this company has its own background. We teach from the top down to the bottom and also have our people travel much in order to get a broad outlook. (Industrial manager, Mexico.)

Executive Selection and Training

My brother and I were both trained in this field and brought some others with us when we arrived from Europe. As for other executives, they must be young, flexible, and capable of being formed; the oldest executive here is thirty-six years old. In promoting people, we look for those who are capable of taking full responsibility, are well coordinated, and can be relied on, though they *may* commit human errors. They also must know Venezuela and be happy here, be part of the community. (Industrial manager, Venezuela.)

A few companies now employ psychological testing when hiring executives and other office personnel, but this is still the exception. Among the desirable personal traits, honesty, initiative, the way in which personal income is used, and sound family background—meaning more often healthy relations at home than origin in a family of high standing—were frequently emphasized.

Aside from the preference for promotion within the company, mentioned earlier, there seemed to be no substantial difference between the criteria for initial selection and those for subsequent promotion of executive personnel. However, a Brazilian bank manager who had formerly taught economics at the local university emphasized that they promote those people who continue their education. They give them enough time to do so and to receive further training either inside the bank or elsewhere. They preferably promote within the company but its expansion has been so fast that they have had to draw some people from other sources. The personal qualities looked for were described as character, personality, efficiency, and "ideas."

Some but not all managers of public enterprises complained about political influences in both selection and promotion, more so at the top level than in the lower echelons of management.

The selection and promotion of executive personnel in

most parts of Latin America remain heavily influenced by family status, political factors, personal acquaintance or recommendation by friends, and other noneconomic considerations which were pointed out in Chapter II. There is as yet little realization of the potential advantages of objective criteria in executive personnel policy on the basis of systematic training and subsequent favorable performance. However, awareness of the need for such criteria has slowly been increasing, especially with greater development-mindedness in some managerial groups.[3]

Executive Training Needs

A question aimed at the perceived importance of training in the efficiency of management [4] elicited a variety of responses again representing to some extent the degree of development in the area concerned and the level of education in the person interviewed. In Venezuela, training ambitions among managers, either for themselves or for their staff, were found to be far more widespread than in various other countries. Some of these ambitions, it is true, seemed to be directed rather uncritically at an imitation of North American management, which, along with Spanish and Central European immigrants, is quite influential in the business life of that country.

Generally a person who had had little formal training himself did not think much of it as a general principle, or had given little thought to it. He tended to associate training chiefly with practical experience in the specific field of

---

[3] United Nations, *op. cit.*, pp. 8–17. Richard S. Roberts, Jr., *Economic Development, Human Skills, and Technical Assistance* (Geneva: International Labour Office, 1962).

[4] "To what extent do you consider efficient management a matter of training?"

enterprise or industry concerned or, at best, with instruction within the company strictly for its own purposes, in a few cases as an obligation for younger executives.

There were, however, exceptions to this rule and some managers who had received no formal training wished they had, or considered it essential for the younger generation. This appeared to apply chiefly to areas which had achieved some degree of industrialization already or showed a dynamic drive toward it. In areas such as Caracas and Mexico City a good many of the managers, especially the younger ones, had received substantial executive training themselves either before or during their conduct of business, and firmly believed in it as an essential requirement for efficient performance on the job as well as for the economic development of their country. This is exemplified by the following two statements:

Conditions of training are not satisfactory here. There is lack of it on two levels: the factory and the administration. Changes are needed in accordance with the kind of enterprise. There is lack of able instructors with experience but also solid academic background. A new conscience of the businessman must be developed with regard to the social function of the enterprise. Most businessmen are men of action—not of education (*preparación.*) For example, there is no market research. Training abroad is necessary, too. United States training is more important for us than inter-American facilities, but we can pass it on to others. (Lawyer and business man, Mexico.)

We have fought for training very insistently. But there is much resistance, especially from those who would need training most. They want immediate results without cost. We use instructors from the firm and from outside. They, too, can learn from the courses they give, and this includes foreign instructors. The human element does not differ much even though habits differ. (Industrial manager, Mexico.)

Training emphasis on *actitud*, rather than *aptitud*, or on the motivational and educational, rather than the purely technical, aspects of managerial efficiency, was recommended in some cases. A number of respondents pointed out that the right natural endowment, such as intelligence, imagination, "push," and emotional maturity, was essential in order to make training effective. But the majority's view can be summed up in the words *el empresario no nace sino se hace* (the enterpriser is made, not born.) A Venezuelan bank executive modified this by saying that the top man is born but that his colleagues must be trained. In particular, the importance of converting some able technicians into administrators and organizers was repeatedly pointed out.[5] A Venezuelan manager added that training *polishes* the able man and that his own company tries to have only executives with college training. Interestingly but perhaps not very realistically, the manager of a small industrial enterprise in Guatemala claimed that management in his country is generally good even though people are not always aware of their own efficiency; they practice it without knowing it, the reason being that in a small country most enterprises are managed by "entrepreneurs" with an *instinct* for management. Even so, he considered training quite important. Another Guatemalan manager pointed out that there are no prepared places for executives there; a trained executive must create a *new* enterprise.

Only a fairly small group interpreted executive training as an essentially academic affair to be left to the universities. The rarity of this view represented in part subjective mistrust toward "theory," and in part the objective scarcity of

[5] See also Banco de México, Departamento de Investigaciones Industriales, *El Empleo de Personal Técnico en la Industria de Transformación* (México, D. F.: 1959), especially Part II.

university facilities for executive training in most of Latin America even now, preceded by almost complete absence of such facilities until a very few years ago.

Another group considered the combination of academic and practical training the ideal arrangement. Some interviewees viewed the university professor with practical business experience as the best kind of instructor. There were some complaints that the really able instructor seldom has enough time to do much teaching. The management courses offered by productivity centers and, in a few cases, by employers' associations were mostly welcomed as a promising beginning, at least, but there were some warnings against "too much talk" or too little intellectual discipline in them, and complaints about the lack of follow-up of short-term training. An industrial manager in Mexico said that he is an enemy of outside courses, regardless of whether they are offered in Mexico City or in Chicago, because people are more inhibited there than within the company and do not absorb things well outside their natural environment. Moreover, he maintained, such courses are a hunting ground for raiders of executive talent.

The concrete purpose of all these facilities, often referred to as *desarrollo gerencial* (managerial development), had seldom been thought about much. It was sometimes expressed, however, as approximation to North American or Western European standards of efficiency, systematic decision-making, avoidance of waste, increase in profit or, more rarely, "industrial thinking," long-range considerations, or active interest in national economic development. The importance of language training was mentioned chiefly by foreign-born interviewees. The technical kinds of training including quality control, accounting, and administrative organization received great emphasis. In some cases, however, more general education in finance, economics, "human relations," social legislation, and history was considered desirable in order to produce a high-caliber executive.

The Asociación Venezolana de Ejecutivos includes *formación espiritual* of the executive in its extensive course program which also comprises marketing, psychology, commercial laws, industrial relations, financing of economic development, accident prevention, and other subjects.[6] Venezuela also has the government-sponsored Instituto Venezolano de Productividad and Instituto Nacional de Cooperación Educativa, which include "the social development of the executive" in their aims. In Mexico IMAN (Instituto Mexicano de Administración de Negocios) now includes some related courses in its curriculum. In Brazil the governmental Banco do Nordeste do Brasil considers it one of its most important functions to train specialists who are to work with private enterprises, especially in industry, on investment projects of developmental interest, and generally to foster entrepreneurial mentality and development-mindedness.

Little spontaneous mention was made in response to this question of executive training as a path to the establishment of *new* enterprises, even though the latter were often mentioned in response to other parts of the questionnaire. In other words, the interviewees associated executive training mainly with relieving the present shortage of trained executives and increasing the administrative efficiency of existing enterprises.

[6] See the publications series of the Asociación, including Ivan Lansberg Henríquez, *El Ejecutivo y su Formación* (Caracas: Asociación Venezolana de Ejecutivos, 1962) and Arturo Uslar Pietri, *Los Hombres de Empresa y la Plaza Pública* (Caracas: Asociación Venezolana de Ejecutivos, 1962).

Thinking of executive training in terms of more successful competition of the firm, however, also appeared to be
rare, especially with reference to the domestic market.
Even a clear association of executive training with cost re-
duction was infrequent. In some extreme cases such training
was interpreted as a costly, unnecessary luxury for a small
firm, or for people operating in an economy where anyone
can sell whatever he is able to produce or import, and
where for an enterprising man money is practically lying
around in the streets. There was some evidence of the attitude, "I am making money anyway, why should I try to
improve?" An interviewee in Northeast Brazil who runs a
combination of industrial, agrarian, and financial enterprises actually boasted that he had never been to school,
though someone had taught him on a *fazenda* (ranch) how
to read and write. Others felt that they were far too busy
for such extra activities, or did not like the idea of being examined like schoolboys.

Among those who had an affirmative approach to executive training, a minority had definite ideas concerning the
level of management on which this would be most important. Most of those who expressed an opinion on this matter felt that the middle executive was the one above all who
should be trained. There was much concern about the absence of a second echelon which could take over when the
chief was away or getting ready to retire. It was also
claimed occasionally that the rarity of a delegation of managerial responsibilities could be explained by the fact that
there was no one to delegate them to; a claim that probably
exaggerated the existing, real problem and became the basis
of rationalizations.

For the lower or younger staff members it was more
often assumed that they were receiving, or had the oppor-

tunity to receive, executive training. The top managers rarely appeared to have considered the possibility that they, too, might still learn something from high-level training other than occasional lectures or seminar meetings. But a Brazilian bank manager with academic background considered training essential precisely at the decision-making level.

Executive Training Abroad

The question of training abroad received mixed reactions. In such areas as Northeast Brazil few managers were able to comment on it in the absence of firsthand experience or knowledge. A sugar producer in that area, however, commented:

I have spent three years in business schools in England and Switzerland but did not really apply my studies here because upon my return I became manager right away succeeding my father. There is not much similarity between European and Brazilian conditions.

In Venezuela, on the other hand, many interviewees had definite experiences and ideas on the subject. Complete rejection of executive training outside the country was quite rare. Unqualified approval was considerably more frequent. The largest group, however, approved the principle with certain reservations. One of them concerned the difference between the technical and the human aspects of management. Several interviewees thought that technical training abroad in engineering, for example, was very valuable and—unless it was excessively specialized—could readily be applied anywhere. On the other hand, training in "human relations," personnel management, sales methods, perhaps even accounting, if based on experiences acquired in dealing with North American or British people, might have few applications in Guatemala or Peru. For similar reasons, the "case method" often used by foreign instructors was viewed skeptically if the cases used were North American, for instance, or even domestic but prepared by foreigners. It was said that with the efficient methods from the North one might easily lose money here. A Venezuelan industrialist claimed that the average North American company which operates there fails to use local know-how and that this failure often costs it much money in labor relations.

Of those who had received training abroad or had associates who had, many, but not all, thus felt that the foreign training was only partly applicable to local conditions or that readjustment problems of some importance arose for trainees upon their return to the home environment, especially after a long absence. It was repeatedly mentioned, however, that this was more true of young men sent abroad at the beginning of their career than of more seasoned executives who already had roots and experience in domestic enterprises *before* going abroad for further training.

Some doubts were expressed whether younger businessmen representing precisely the dynamic type could really be expected to spend years abroad for training when there was so much to do at home. It is true that some of those who had reservations added that a trainee usually does come back to his country with many new stimuli to his executive thinking, and that in most cases he is able to make the appropriate adjustment to local conditions.[7] It was also claimed, however, that some who had received training abroad did nothing with it after their return. An industrialist in El Salvador pointed out that readjustment is often delayed because the trainees abroad have not been taught

[7] Compare Michael L. Hoffman, "Development Needs the Business Man," *Lloyds Bank Review* (April, 1963).

psychological adaptation. A Brazilian bank manager claimed, however, that there is far greater difficulty with the boys coming out of the *Brazilian* universities, who think they know everything already and often use this belief as a reason to go into government service.

Among the factors requiring a modification of foreign experiences in order to make them usable under local conditions, the assumptions of "bigness," standardization, mechanization, and executive division of labor in North American management training, in contrast with the small markets and enterprises in most of Latin America, were mentioned repeatedly. European experiences were thought to be more readily applicable there. Other differences pointed out included the human factor in handling semiliterate workers from a recent rural background or unsophisticated customers who had no concept of choosing systematically, the absence of efficient and inexpensive credit facilities, the influence of political pull in doing business, corruption in the government, social unrest, religious influences, and the frequency of monopoly or else cutthroat competition.

The use of foreign instructors in the country concerned was mostly approved of as a more efficient and less expensive way of utilizing foreign experience. Reservations were made, however, concerning the personality traits and adaptability required of a foreign instructor; for example, his ability to demonstrate specific problems and solutions under unaccustomed economic and cultural conditions. Another reservation referred to the minimum length of time which a foreign instructor needs to spend in the country in order to be really effective. An industrial manager in Mexico claimed that foreign instructors are effective only on a *high* level of management; on the lower levels, animosity can easily develop as a result of North American at-

titudes of racial superiority or constant complaints of
instructors about Latin American "inefficiency."

By way of experiment the interviewer occasionally
raised the question whether inter-American training facilities for executive personnel should be established. Hardly
anybody had had definite thoughts on this subject, though
some respondents thought vaguely that it might be a good
idea. In Guatemala and El Salvador the progress of the
Central American Common Market had made such thinking somewhat more specific than in the other countries
visited.

In summary, not only is the selection and promotion of
executives in Latin America often lacking in objective criteria at this point, but executive training, too, is still rather
haphazard. This applies both to facilities available and
actual instruction, with considerable differences according
to the area and managerial generation concerned. In ap-
pointing and promoting executives there is still an interplay
of family contacts and influences, practical experience on
the job, perceived personal traits such as "character,"
domestic training of either academic or nonacademic types,
and instruction abroad if adapted to local conditions. A
combination of practical and academic training is highly
valued. As a general trend, awareness of needs for systematic training of persons with basic ability for management
appears to be on the increase, though concrete association
of such needs with competitive effectiveness or the economic development of the nation remains rare.

IV

Management Aims
and Satisfactions

HOW do those selected and promoted to high-ranking positions in management in the ways just described interpret the aims of management and the chief satisfactions and dissatisfactions of managerial activity?

Aims of Management

After some queries about the main activity, age, and ownership structure of the enterprise and the interviewee's function in it, the following question was asked: "How would you describe the principal aim that guides the management of this enterprise?"

Responses to this question were extremely varied. Surprise at being asked this kind of question was generally greatest in the least developed areas, especially in smaller firms. The respondent either had not thought about such matters at all or had taken for granted that the aim of management was to keep the company going gainfully, and nothing but that. An occasional, somewhat related answer referred to intended superiority over all the other competitors.

In more developed areas many responses showed that more elaborate thinking had been done on the subject. In these cases the answer was often in the nature of "to obtain profit, of course, but this is not all." A Mexican industrialist, for example, commented:

My purpose is to work, to create new industry and, through it, a higher standard of living. Not just money. If a business is well planned, profit will come anyway. If I wanted nothing but money I'd just be a money-lender and charge crazy interest rates.

Similarly, an industrial manager in Venezuela said:

Money is not the chief aim. Both my brother and I had plenty of it before we started this concern. Our aim is a good, strong industrial group which is basically adapted to the economy of the country and is not a parasite but makes a contribution. For this reason we don't go into land purchases, for instance.

Some answers were presented in such terms as "to provide quality products at low cost," "to provide employment and income for some of the people in this community," or, less frequently, "to make a contribution to the industrial development of the country." A Mexican banker and promoter said that he aims at industrial diversification, only promotes industries that are in the long-run national interest, and does not consider unnecessary consumer industries or amusements no matter how profitable, even though the financial success of a company is "revealing."

Another Mexican banker answered the entire question largely in terms of national needs:

There are several goals to be considered. First, to make savings more popular and with it, investment. The number of savers is still small; we want to increase it constantly. Second, agrarian financing for a growing number of small landowners. But there are problems in it because their education level is precarious; they know nothing of credit or techniques and need protection against cheating. Third, industrialization, and a crusade for greater and more diversified exports.

Despite many complaints about underemployment of existing industrial capacity, progress or expansion of the company was mentioned frequently as the principal aim of management. This also came out with even greater frequency in response to a later question about investment intentions. Explicit association of such expansion with national development needs was infrequent. On the other hand, high income for stockholders or managers was rarely mentioned spontaneously, though it was probably taken for granted by many. Some managers whose companies had established medical, housing, or welfare facilities for their workers answered in corresponding terms. An industrial manager in Mexico claimed that his company had very special characteristics:

It is the *social* aspect of industrial relations that matters most here. We have been long supplying food, transport, housing, schools, and stores to our workers and they share the gains of the company.

Management Aims and Satisfactions

In general, the principal aim was expressed in the form not of long-range but of immediate objectives. An approximation to long-range considerations was offered by the Venezuelan businessman who answered: "Defending the private-enterprise system by making it meaningful." A public-enterprise manager in Mexico felt that private enterprise had gone through an adventurer-entrepreneur phase but that more permanent aims prevailed now. The manager of a producers' cooperative in Mexico described its permanent aim as lowering the operational costs in distribution and having the members save the difference. This was thought of as a service both to the members and to the public, and he emphasized that the cooperative had no profit aim even though it *could* make profit. Broad social goals of the enterprise such as jobs and stability were also listed by a number of managers in long-range terms.

For my private convenience, I would not live here, the political situation being what it is. But I am fulfilling a duty. My partners feel the same way. Without us, things would turn even worse. (European-born industrial manager, Venezuela.)

A substantial number of answers were given in technical terms, especially by executives with such backgrounds as engineering or architecture. These answers included increasing the quality or variety of the product, acquiring the latest kind of machinery, improving the plant organization and so forth.

In explaining why money, while necessary, was not the primary objective of management, an executive in Mexico said that his father had never worked for the sake of money since he had more already than he could ever spend. A more definite connection was revealed by others between the level of education and the range of thinking about management aims. Those managers who had experienced little education had rarely thought ahead sufficiently to be able to answer the question under discussion in a meaningful way, and sometimes were bewildered by it. Especially did this apply to those in charge of smaller companies. Business was seen by many of them as pretty much taking care of itself; why strain one's brain about the future, with the only possible exception of external disturbances such as a runaway inflation or social radicalism?

At the other extreme there were a small number of highly educated, sophisticated, and socially responsible managers who tried to convert their fellow businessmen to their own views. An example is offered by the following statement:

In the first place one must understand perfectly that the function of the executive is not to supply to the capitalist a rather high yield, and that the index of his success is not measured exactly by the rising curve of the economic indices of the enterprise. The executive has a goal and a cause. His goal is to get ahead of himself as a result of integration of his own personality. . . . The real asset of the enterprise is the human element. This is precisely the cause for which the executive works: human betterment and social justice. Human betterment to be achieved through economic effort, work designed to raise the standard of living through greater productivity, effort for systematic organization of economic resources in order to achieve the last aim of prosperity, abundance for everybody.

The executive, in order to perform, must love. He cannot limit himself to the sharing of benefits without knowing how to share the joy of life and work. To love is to give, to give of oneself, and wealth does not consist in what one has got but in what one gives. Wealth is not to be found in capital but in service.[1]

[1] Ivan Lansberg Henríquez, interview in *El Nacional,* Caracas, Dec. 18, 1962; also his paper on "Management: An Idea in Action," (mimeo., Feb., 1963); and *The Executive, The Corporation and*

Management Aims and Satisfactions

Only a small minority related their own activity or that of their firm clearly to development trends or needs of the country. In fact, the greater were the objective development needs of an area, the fewer the enterprise managers who seemed to think in those terms. The prevailing attitude might best be summed up by saying that the majority of the managers interviewed had a vague feeling that there was, or should be, more to the conduct of an enterprise than merely keeping it profitable, but that perception of any definite aims or tasks in long-range terms, as a contribution to the economic and social advancement of the country, remained confined to a sophisticated minority.[2]

By way of an appendix to this section, there follows a rather illuminating statement made by a managerial executive of an important public enterprise in Mexico regarding the current development stages of business groups with the corresponding management aims:

In this country there are three groups of businessmen, with different attitudes:

The *first* faces no risk regarding the demand for his product. He normally can plan his investment regardless, for example in the production of beer and bottles. His opinions on development have effective channels to express themselves politically. The development of these companies is tuned to national development and they can wait, even absorb losses or else pass them on to the State. This applies chiefly to business in the large centers.

The *second* group is that of the *beginning* entrepreneurs and it is quite different. For them things don't work well yet. They

Social Progress (Caracas: Asociación Venezolana de Ejecutivos, 1964).

[2] Compare Daniel R. Fusfeld, "Heterogony of Entrepreneurial Goals," *Explorations in Entrepreneurial History*, Vol. 9, No. 1 (Oct., 1956).

use promoters from the outside, have little resources themselves. They expect immediate profit especially from new products, such as appliances, in the interest of capital formation, but they also need bank credit or other help. They suffer frequent losses. Much depends for them on government contracts. This group is very promising but has had no time yet to think in terms of economic development. The Common Market is vivid in the minds of the first but not the second group. This latter group needs fiscal protection and counseling.

Third comes the forgotten man. He interprets industry as improvements of handicrafts. Especially is this true in the provinces. He works for the local market and is interested in *local* development, has no economic viewpoint. He is fearful of foreign competition. The State can destroy him, too. He thinks more of survival than of profit or investment. This group is very numerous, if you think of tailors or silversmiths, for instance, but it is not important insofar as its total investment is concerned. From it, however, come the best entrepreneurs! Just look at the shoe industry. They depend heavily on protectionism, though. But this group is very promising because Mexico must develop according to the European not the North American pattern.

The difference in geographic conditions is extremely important in this country. Monterrey, for example, is developed. Economic development is largely a regional problem. Some parts of the country are still Spanish colonies, in a sense.

Managerial Satisfactions and Dissatisfactions

In comparison with the expressed principal aims of managerial activity, what are the chief satisfactions of managers in a newly developing economy, and what are the main sources of discontent? This was the subject of the following questions:

(a) "What are the chief satisfactions which you find in managerial activity?"

(b) "Are there any dissatisfactions?"

On the whole, managers were very eager to talk about such questions even though they were of a more personal nature than the entire rest of the questionnaire. It was clear that many interviewees had thought before about related issues or, at least, felt that they should have thought about them, from their own point of view, and that the interview offered a welcome stimulus to do so.

Theoretically it would have been conceivable that the predominant answer to the first part of the question would be "money" or "high income." Actually the response was far more complex. Leaving aside some who were taken by surprise and were too puzzled to give a coherent answer, only a small minority mentioned money or income first. However, a good many took financial rewards for granted in some way or, at least, included them among their standards of satisfaction.

Many more commented that the high income resulting from their managerial or business activity was pleasant, desirable, or reassuring, but that it constituted a mere starting point or precondition for satisfactions of more important kinds:

Profit is not decisive. Personal factors are more important—to *do* something with life. We began to produce with national resources and now we use 95 per cent domestic materials. We had confidence in our government and in the consumer needs of our people as economic factors in our field and want to help the mechanization and automation of industry here. Other than this we have no "aim." (Industrial manager, Mexico.)

I am a man who is *inquieto* and impassioned for his country. I am financially well off but am not interested in money. I believe in Mexico, have very many friends, and enjoy my life. (Lawyer and businessman, Mexico.)

I am a man with drive—I hail from Catalonia. I like to build up something new. I suffer from lack of people I can trust, and of investors, but I always have some new projects going. (Industrial manager, Guatemala.)

Several commented that money was not an important yardstick because they or their families had more already than they could ever spend for personal purposes. Family traditions and roots in the kind of enterprise which they headed were felt to be the decisive factor of satisfaction in a number of cases.

Growth of the company and the earning of profits required to finance such growth were mentioned repeatedly as the mainstay of managerial satisfaction. It will be shown, however, that this was usually only one aspect of the satisfactions derived from meeting a challenge, doing the job itself, or fulfilling the desire to "create," to build up a large enterprise, to promote, to acquire modern facilities, to offer new products to the consumer, or—less frequently—to make a contribution to the industrial development of the country or to high employment and standard of living. Creativity and social utility emerged in various ways as an important driving force and, when fulfilled, a major source of satisfaction.

As a boy I was a shift boss in a gold and silver mine. It was a soulless occupation. On this job here, I handle a noble product which serves humanity. As a boy I wanted to be a captain of industry. I did not quite get there, but I am making a certain amount of money without hurting anyone. I have everybody as a friend. I am a spiritualist by religion; I believe in general laws of the universe. My religion says, "You should not be materialistic." I want to be liked, then I'll be better off financially, too. (Manager, industrial company, Mexico.)

Financial and personal success is very important to me, but I must also feel that I am making a civic contribution. But the majority of businessmen do not think this way, are lacking in social sense. (President of an employers' group, Mexico.)

Among the managers of public enterprises there were repeated expressions of a related satisfaction that came from working directly for the welfare of the country, a satisfaction which was felt to make up for possible factors of a less favorable nature such as lower pay in certain categories.

Personally, I prefer public management. Many people think that public management is badly administered; I want to prove the opposite. Our incentives are just as good as those of private enterprise. The government has a complementary part in making up for many deficiencies of private enterprise. It is more difficult to manage a public enterprise, but it can be done and then produces a chain reaction in creating good will. We try, though, to avoid political interference at any price. (Manager, public enterprise, Mexico.)

Closely related to creativity needs was a desire for independence, which was clearly manifested by owner-managers but also led to the widespread claim on the part of hired managers that *they*, not the owners, run the show and derive much satisfaction from this decisive role. In some cases this claim was at odds with evidence from other sources regarding the actual distribution of power within the company, but this did not impair the strength of the aspiration to be independent and, thereby, truly creative.

I like independence, freedom of action. I like the problems, too. When there are none, I'll retire! (Industrialist, Mexico.)

I like to be busy and creative, to put together the financial, industrial, and human elements. Once an enterprise is going, I turn over the management to others and dispose of details. (Industrialist, Mexico.)

Construction constantly transforms everybody; it is always different, one always plans new things. (Manager, construction firm, Mexico.)

The feeling of having conquered successfully a past challenge rooted in the newness of the enterprise or in other difficulties, or of having to keep conquering the emerging challenges continuously, was listed frequently in various forms as a factor of satisfaction.

To carry through the program, to carry out a constructive activity, to apply foreign experiences to Mexico insofar as applicable, to hold the product prices down through savings to the producers; to carry out an idea. (Manager, producers' cooperative, Mexico.)

Some but not all of the challenges listed specifically were implicit in the nature of an insufficiently developed economy; for example, lack of education among the workers or shortages of transportation facilities, difficulties which, it was felt, the management of the company had successfully struggled against. In other cases a related source of managerial satisfaction was expressed in terms of doing the job itself; for example, the constant stimulation and interest that are implicit in supervising people, selling goods, and talking to customers.

It is a difficult job with many adverse moments during recessions, in particular. During prosperity it is pleasant work which makes a contribution to the national economy. I am an economist and *as such* find bank work very interesting. I am the "father confessor" for many people and get insights into the human psyche. (Bank manager, Venezuela.)

Cotton is like a beautiful woman who gets more interesting every day. The problems never repeat themselves. (Manager, commercial company, Mexico.)

An industrial manager in Mexico said that he personally feels the strain of work and prefers loafing, but that he feels an obligation to live up to the moral compulsion to make an effort in the interest of the growth of the company.

Relations with associates and other people on the business level were mentioned frequently as a factor of managerial satisfaction, but were listed in other cases as a cause of discontent. "Associates" meant sometimes the executive staff, at other times the workers and employees in general; in a good many cases it referred to close relations among members of one family who were all active in the enterprise, usually on the managerial level. A financial manager in Venezuela said:

I feel satisfied when I see a contented and happy personnel here. Also when I can fulfill my "mission" and ambition to grow. These two things go together. I feel dissatisfied when we have failed to give good service according to my own judgment.

The European-born manager of a financial enterprise in Chile (reinterview, 1963) said that his dealings with the Board of Directors are most satisfactory because they are men of "European culture," though not necessarily Europeans. The manager of a construction firm in Mexico spoke of the satisfaction coming from

the living together of a group of people, the sense of obligation among them, their conviction about what they all are doing, once the physical necessities have been satisfied.

Another one said:

My satisfaction is "nationalist." I want to see this big enterprise managed entirely by Mexicans, and also to know that the foreign investment in it is good for Mexico. I don't like, though, to have to be apologetic about this foreign ownership. (Industrial manager, Mexico.)

Enterprise in Latin America

Interestingly, the same man said later in the interview:

I am for unrestricted foreign investment, including oil. The American and British companies were stupid to hand oil over to Cárdenas. They should have offered him candies, not resistance.

Paternalist feelings toward the personnel were found to be fairly frequent, especially in the least developed areas.

My brothers and I were the first in this industry. Our objectives are not only economic but social, and the latter are much more important. For me the enterprise is a family. Everybody including the workers is equally interested in it. More employment and welfare for everyone in the company, with continuing training and better wages, gives us satisfaction. (Industrial manager, El Salvador.)

In all probability the workers in many cases did not actually hold the feelings of affection toward the managers which the latter assumed to exist, but such possible discrepancies did not seem to interfere with the managerial satisfactions felt or rationalizations.[3]

As for dissatisfactions, some interviewees said that they could not think of any at all (an industrial manager in Venezuela said, "Nothing—I do only what I like to do") but many more had some to register. To begin with, the same factors that were listed as satisfying when fulfilled became sources of discontent when frustrated. This was true of growth ambitions, profit yields, wishes of independence, creative urges, challenges encountered, expectations regarding the nature of the job, and desires for friendly, mutually

[3] Compare José Medina Echavarría, *Consideraciones Sociológicas Sobre el Desarrollo Económico de América Latina* (Santiago: United Nations Economic and Social Council, 1962), mimeo., pp. 32ff., section on "Paternalism, Anxiety, and Impersonal Organization." English version, *Social Aspects of Economic Development in Latin America*, Vol. II (Paris: Unesco, 1963), pp. 39ff.

understanding relations with the personnel and other people. In particular, it was pointed out in some cases that the family roots of an enterprise may not only limit its financial scope but may lead to problems in family relations. One interviewee in Mexico listed as his main source of discontent, "to have to *work*, and the number of things I have to do." A small businessman in Chile stated:

We are independent, but my wife and I have to work from 8:00 A.M. to 8:00 P.M. and then prepare work for the next day. I fall into my bed, read a little, then sleep. On Sunday I often sleep, too. We see nothing of the beauties of Chile. Our world is the apartment and the shop.

In a more general way, the performance of labor was a fairly frequent source of complaints. This was true primarily of the educational level and training of the workers and, in a lesser degree, of the effect of labor unions when they are guided by adverse political or ideological influences. The prevailing attitude of managers in these cases was that the worker in the country concerned is intelligent and learns fast but that unions or agitators may prevent him from doing his best. Fear of radical influences or outright communism was a recurrent, but by no means universal, source of discontent.

Complaints about government and politics, on the other hand, were extremely common, even though the typical complexion of such complaints varied considerably from one country to another, as will be shown in Chapter VI. Corruption on many or all levels of government, inefficiency, red tape and paper work, the prevalence of political pull, legal complexities or uncertainties, competition from state enterprises, and instability or indecision in public life were cited time and again. A few interviewees added, however, that business often *asks* for specific kinds of state intervention. An industrial manager in El Salvador also complained about lack of understanding on the part of many capitalists who still have an agrarian mentality and think a factory is like a coffee plantation.

In summary, the aims of managers turned out to be only partly financial and more so for their enterprises than for themselves. In a large degree these aims were focused at stability or expansion of the enterprise, the expression of creative urges, or a contribution to social and economic improvement. Company profit as the basis of high individual incomes offered by no means an adequate explanation of managerial satisfactions or discontents. More indirectly, as the basis of company growth, it came somewhat closer to the explanation of such feelings. Even so, a variety of additional factors such as the desire for independence and creativity, the conquest of a challenge, the nature of the managerial job as such, relations with associates and others, and political and governmental influences must be taken into account in order to understand the managerial attitudes in question. To this must be added the perception of competition, market limitations, investment, and productivity, which will be discussed in the following chapter.

V

Competition, Productivity, and Investment

IN comparison with the perceived aims and satisfactions of management, how do Latin American enterprise managers view their actual behavior on the job, and how do they relate it to the economic development process? To what extent do they perceive the prevailing conditions of competition, market size, productivity, and investment as either limiting or favorable?

Competition and Market Size

Ways of thinking concerning competition and market limitations were revealed by interviewees partly in response to the question about managerial satisfactions and discontents, especially the latter, and partly in answering various other questions. Attitudes toward competition were more ambivalent than attitudes regarding most other issues raised in the interviews. The abstract principle of competition was usually approved heartily, especially in countries such as Venezuela where the influence of North American ideology is strong. There were some instances of enterprise managers saying that they welcomed "constructive" competitors or that they needed "normal" competition in order to be kept on their toes.

Such responses, however, were overshadowed by mistrustful interpretation of competition as a bothersome source of discontent, usually leading to the conclusion that "excessive" competition, at least, should be restrained either by private or by public action.[1] This especially applied to fears of superior foreign competition, and to the frequent belief that competition in general was an expensive luxury for an underdeveloped country.

A financial manager in Venezuela claimed that:

. . . the Latin American can compete only when he is furious. He interprets competition as personal aggression. This is why there is so little business competition here!

[1] An Argentinian management expert comments: "We all know from experience what inefficiency is caused by the obstructionism of the businessman toward the release of certain data because he is afraid of competition, and what disastrous results come from bureaucratic carelessness which mistrusts the statements of businessmen and in many cases acts as judge with insufficient knowledge of situations or under selfish pressure from rival groups—groups which, because of their respective backgrounds, are only capable of seeing immediate effects without being interested in the implications of any measure which they demand in the firm belief that it is just." Juan Llamazares, *Empresas Modernas: Ensayos sobre Dirección y Organización* (Buenos Aires: Instituto Argentino de Relaciones Industriales, 1955), p. 16.

On the other hand, very many interviewees commented that competition did not bother them in practice, either because of monopolistic advantages or understandings they enjoyed or because of the readiness of markets in a rapidly growing population to absorb practically all the products offered no matter from how many sources they came. A Mexican banker claimed, "We are all friends and there is no foul play."

Strangely enough, belief in a pre-established growing market for consumers' goods, at least, was often coupled within the same business population (and sometimes the same individuals) with an equally firm belief in the existence of intrinsic limitations to the size of markets as a result of smallness of the country or the ignorance and poverty of the rank and file. Such reservations were frequent especially in response to a question asked about any recent progress in productivity (to be discussed later). The smallness of the national market was perceived by many as a kind of law of nature against which nothing could be done. Productivity, often confounded with high production, was considered pointless in such a situation: "why should I make more goods than I do if there are few more buyers around than I have got now?" [2] Competition abroad was usually not even considered insofar as manufactured goods were concerned.

In other words, the prevailing attitude assumed that the minority who constituted an effective market was eager to buy almost anything that was offered, and that this minority would keep increasing in absolute terms with the constant growth of the population, but that the rest of the

[2] "The owner seeks essentially to make a living rather than maximize profits." "Use of Accounting as an Aid to Management in Underdeveloped Countries," George Ronson, *Industrialization and Productivity*, Bulletin No. 1, United Nations (1958), p. 60.

people, especially in the countries with a large Indian population, might as well not exist insofar as the national consumers' market was concerned.

Concepts of Productivity

To what extent do Latin American managers relate the market size, the competitive situation, and their own function to the productivity performance of the enterprise? In what sense have they got any definite concept of productivity? What is their perception of the responses of their workers to productivity measures? These questions were the subject of further items in the questionnaire.[3]

To begin with, only a minority of the managers interviewed had a reasonably clear-cut concept of productivity, with great variations according to the area, for example, between São Paulo and Northeast Brazil. Some interviewees, especially in smaller businesses, were obviously unfamiliar with the very concept of productivity, even though they did not say so openly. Many more answered the question about progress in productivity in terms of *production* by saying, for example, that the output of the company was much higher now than it had been three years before.

When the question was explained by using such terms as "efficiency" or "output per man-hour," the answer tended to be vaguely optimistic. Very few firms seemed to have concrete data on such progress; the managers neither knew them nor responded by pressing a button, calling an aide, and asking him to get the figures from the files. There were,

[3] (1) "Has the level of productivity in this enterprise increased during recent years or not?"

(2) "How do the workers react to measures for higher productivity?"

however, some notable exceptions from this prevailing response.

In most cases the managers thought that progress in efficiency had been made during the preceding period. Sometimes this statement was made with great assurance even though no exact data were available. In other cases it was said that some progress had been made but not nearly enough. A minority stated that efficiency had remained stable, and a few said that it had actually gone down as a result of rising costs, in particular. A sugar producer in Northeast Brazil claimed that pay increases had *lowered* productivity, as their workers were uneducated and saw no reason to go out of their way in order to earn more than what little they were used to.

Insufficient progress of productivity, however, was not necessarily blamed on the workers. Antiquated equipment or external impediments such as government restrictions were frequently quoted both by the group that saw little or no progress achieved and by the group that did think that substantial progress had been made. An industrial manager in Guatemala claimed that lack of a large market forced his firm into excessive diversification which impeded productivity. The most frequently quoted obstacle, however, referred to governmental processes. In Venezuela, in particular, there were widespread complaints about lack of clarity concerning future nationalization intentions, a lack which was seen as impeding any incentive to improve the plants or equipment. In every country visited political favoritism, nepotism, red tape, or outright corruption were mentioned by many, though by no means all, interviewees as obstacles to higher productivity in their own enterprise. We are not, of course, judging the objective merits of such explanations.

Credit for improvements of productivity achieved, on

the other hand, was quite rarely given to governmental development policies and was usually claimed for the company management concerned. This applied, for example, to the introduction of improved machinery or the use of foreign experts. The government was also blamed more indirectly for obstacles to higher productivity resulting from inflationary trends, such as the erosion of working capital and the impossibility of reliable calculation under inflationary conditions.

Other external impediments to rising productivity which were mentioned with some frequency referred to market limitations. This applied in some cases to the perceived smallness of the domestic market which has been mentioned earlier. In other cases the blame was put on foreign markets, either in terms of international price fluctuations or in those of superior competition from other countries. Only a few interviewees perceived productivity as a possible remedy for such limitations.

It must be repeated, however, that the majority felt in a general way, at least, that progress in productivity had been made. Spontaneous credit for such achievements was rarely given to the workers, not surprisingly so in areas where authoritarian traditions remain strong in the relations between employer and worker. New equipment and successful selling methods were mentioned far more frequently. When a question about workers' subjective reactions to productivity measures was asked, however, the prevailing response of the interviewees was favorable. Nearly everywhere the managers felt that the worker in their respective country is very intelligent and learns fast, and some claimed that their workers were proud to work with new machines. Such emphasis was especially frequent in Chile, Brazil, and Mexico but was not lacking in the other countries either.

Productivity and the Worker

At the same time it was pointed out repeatedly that the worker mostly came from a rural, in some regions Indian, background, that he was poorly prepared and in certain areas typically illiterate when he entered the factory, that he was lacking in *cultura* and responsibility, that he tended to "forget" instructions, that absenteeism and turnover—often resulting from sickness, malnutrition, poor housing, disrupted family conditions, gambling, or drinking—were widespread, and that the company had to familiarize him with the simplest mechanical processes, though he was capable enough of catching on to them promptly. The head of a Mexican employers' group stated that productivity is still in a very backward stage precisely *because* of cheap labor; higher wages along with workers' *and* managers' education on productivity are required.

This, it is true, was not a typical attitude. Association of high wages with high productivity was rare. A more widespread managerial view characterized the enterprises as being high-cost producers despite low wages; the workers were admittedly getting very little money but were seen as being worth even less in terms of their productive performance. If high wages should be paid at some future date, this could materialize only *after* labor productivity had gone up. Only a small minority said that the worker wanted to have a share in the yield of improved procedures and would cooperate if he felt assured of such a share.

It was pointed out in various areas that unemployment, both formal and informal, was high and that legal minimum wages often were not enforced, but at the same time that it was very difficult to find skilled labor for technological improvements. Complaints about lack of elementary education as an impediment to rise in productivity and quality of work were frequent, especially in areas with a large Indian population or widespread rural illiteracy. A Mexican industrialist said:

Workers have not been taught to produce more in order to earn more. They'll never understand it, they are just workers. If they understood it they would be more.

And a Guatemalan plantation owner and real-estate man commented:

On my plantation, I am a dictator. Whoever complains is thrown out, even if it involves a whole group. Although there are too many people, there are not enough Indians available now for the work to be done. The Indian only wants to eat, has no other ambitions.

A merchant in Guatemala felt that the efficiency level was rather low as a result of educational limitations, that it was very hard to get good sales people, and that there was an honesty problem with the "smart" ones. Others, however, pointed to an incipient change in generations of workers, the younger ones being better prepared and more ambitious.

Complaints about hostile reactions of workers to productivity measures, on the other hand, were fairly rare. Many managers characterized their workers as docile or cooperative, although a Mexican textile manufacturer claimed that the introduction of new machinery had at first met with determined opposition from the workers and their union. This applied both to the initial time-and-motion studies and to the dismissal of workers, but subsequent "education" had changed the workers' attitude. Other interviewees felt that the initial response to changes was *inevitably* guided by mistrust or fear, especially fear of losing one's job or having to work much harder, and that make-work tendencies were not always easy to uproot, but that in general the workers soon got accustomed to new arrangements.

Some enterprise managers were very emphatic about the need to *explain* things to workers or to assure them that company growth would mean for them continued employment and prestige. But other managers tended to assume that the workers just did not have the education necessary to *understand* what was going on, and that all that mattered was to get them into the habit of doing things the new way.[4] Real knowledge or exploration of the workers' mind appeared to be quite rare, as was the realization that labor attitudes might depend in a large degree on management behavior past and present. Here again there were a few examples to the contrary. The head of an industrial company in Chile when reinterviewed in 1963 proudly pointed out that they were now employing industrial sociologists from Europe and the United States in order to explore workers' responses to productivity measures, though this had led to some unnecessary misunderstandings with the union.

Paternalist responses of managers to the question about workers' behavior were not infrequent if not necessarily realistic. Perhaps it should be emphasized that we are discussing here the image which managers hold regarding the

[4] Compare Walter Galenson (ed.), *Labor and Economic Development* (New York: John Wiley and Sons, 1959), Introduction by Galenson. Also Wilbert E. Moore, *Industrialization and Labor* (Ithaca, N.Y.: Cornell University Press, 1951), especially Part II on Mexico. See also W. E. Moore and A. S. Feldman (eds.), *Labor Commitment and Social Change in Developing Areas* (New York: Social Science Research Council, 1960); Charles A. Myers, "The American System of Industrial Relations: Is It Exportable?" Industrial Relations Research Association, *Proceedings of the 15th Annual Meeting*, 1963.

responses of their workers to productivity measures, not the actual attitudes of workers as they might emerge from direct interviewing of a cross section of workers. Quite a number of managers perceived the workers as trusting them like parents and for *this* reason not manifesting any hostile reaction to changes and innovations in the plant. A public-enterprise manager in Mexico said disapprovingly that in certain cases the state tended to be even more paternalist than private enterprise. A Venezuelan industrialist, on the other hand, thought that the businessman must be both a schoolteacher and a family father for his workers in teaching them social and human values. Another one said:

If you know how to handle them you can get anything from them, much more easily so than from Europeans. They are like children—they want to be treated kindly.

Generally, however, paternalist interpretations of workers' responses to productivity measures and of industrial relations in general appeared to be slowly weakening and to be considerably rarer among the younger generation of managers than among the older. Some interviewees deplored the survival of paternal attitudes and wanted to see them replaced by a businesslike relationship as soon as possible.

Hostile reactions among managers to social-security legislation likewise appeared to be declining. Its bureaucratic administration was heavily criticized but the institution itself seemed to be seen increasingly as a kind of insurance against uncontrollable radicalism.

References to radical agitation, though, were fairly frequent in every country, with distinct regional differences. Managers, in other words, tended to think that their workers were intelligent and cooperative by nature but were inexperienced and credulous in ideological matters, and that their original cooperative attitude might be swayed into indifference or outright hostility under the influence of Communist or radical agitators. Such managerial doubts or fears generally were not directed at labor unions as such but only at those unions which were seen as being dominated by demagogic politicians.

A number of interviewees, it is true, commented with a kind of embarrassed pride that their workers had no union organization. Some added that their workers had been treated so well by the company—for example, through payment of wages above the legal minimum or through free medical services or housing—that they felt no urge to form a union. In any case, unions were seen as obstacles to productivity measures only when dominated by a hostile political ideology.

Productivity and the Manager

Views of higher productivity as primarily a task for management were seldom expressed in a spontaneous way, except for occasional complaints about the lack of efficient executives especially on the plant level, who knew how to utilize efficiently all the available manpower. As has been pointed out in Chapter II, the need for better training of executives ranked rather high among the preoccupations of managers in many areas. Direct association of such training with greater productivity of their enterprises, however, was limited to a few managers mostly with foreign training or background who, indeed, were interested in very advanced methods of productivity management.

In other words, the perception of high productivity as a result to be achieved largely through the efforts and skills of the managers themselves in such respects as production techniques, executive organization, and industrial relations was found to be fairly rare or, at best, focused on the occasional employment of foreign consultants. A Mexican manager said that his firm had obtained good results from improving the productivity level with expert advice, then hiring young executives who would avoid the old errors. Another mentioned resistance from supervisors who were difficult to convince of new procedures.[5]

[5] "All the functions that make higher productivity possible are the responsibility of the entrepreneurs and within their province. On the other hand, our people and government must repudiate as antipatriotic any attempt of the unions that tends to avoid or restrict the efforts and investments of business designed to improve productivity and through it, consumer prices, merely because some workers' groups from specific unions may be exposed to unemployment. . . . It is the apparent inertia on the part of both employers and workers, the quite natural and human tendency to accept as good everything traditional and to decline any change that implies doubled effort or the recognition of new values, to which we are addressing this message."—Heriberto Vidales, speech to *Confederación Patronal de la República Mexicana* (mimeo.), Nov. 8, 1961. A statement of principles by the same organization says, "The increase of productivity must be the result of the common effort of the employer, the worker, and the State; it being the responsibility of the employer to create the necessary conditions in order to raise production without imparing the interests of the worker." (*Declaración de Principios*, p. 7.) A young Argentine businessman judges his fellow managers as follows: "The Argentine manager does not doubt that most of his own workers are skillful, alert, adaptable, and creative. But most managers believe that workers are unwilling or unable to apply such gifts to useful (industrial) purposes. Therefore, all blame for the nation's political, economic, and social troubles is put on labor and indirectly on government for fomenting the workers' natural faults and indolence. In industrial and business circles, there seems to be a lack of awareness that at least part of the responsibility for the retardation of Argentine industrial development is as much attributable to the employers' past and present mistakes as it is to labor and government." Tomás Roberto Fillol, *Social Factors in Economic Development: The Argentine Case* (Cambridge, Mass.: M.I.T. Press, 1961), p. 74. For comparison, Frederick Harbison and Charles A. Myers, *Management in the Industrial World* (New York: McGraw-Hill, 1959), especially Chaps. 2, 5, and (on Chile) 9.

Competition, Productivity, Investment

Actually, cost accounting and inventory control are still fairly rare. The *contadores* mostly confine themselves to bookkeeping and are rarely equipped to keep track of the financial structure of their company. Not many managers know how long goods have been on stock and how much this costs them. When business is poor, expenses are cut down—not necessarily in the right place. A bank executive in Venezuela complained that whenever the staff has to be reduced they lose the best persons because they are the highest-paid.

Likewise, direct association of higher productivity on the company level with faster progress in national economic development was infrequent. So was any consideration of possible discrepancies between efficiency on the company level and productivity in a broader socioeconomic sense. Even among those who had a relatively clear concept of productivity, the latter was mostly thought of only as a device to obtain higher profits and expansion of the company, and in some cases perhaps as a kind of competitive game. The thought that higher productivity of numerous enterprises could make a contribution to the wealth of the nation and its position in the international economy, had occurred only to a sophisticated minority. The national need for greater productivity in certain specific areas of economic life, especially agriculture, was mentioned repeatedly, however.

The head of an industrial association in Brazil felt that under inflation there could be no favorable attitude in the nation toward productivity; some large enterprises know modern scientific management but the medium and small firms have a negative attitude toward any productivity effort: "Inflation is more powerful than any talk, so why make an effort?" He was confident that with stabilization a new attitude would arise.

The social and psychological aspects of efficient performance sometimes enter into the discussion more indirectly as part of the managers' general views of the human element in enterprise and national development. But productivity as such still is a meaningful concept only to a minority of enterprise managers, and systematic implementation of this concept is even rarer. To the extent that productivity is understood, most managers are optimistic about the progress recently achieved or underway. Their view of workers' responses to such improvements is somewhat contradictory. On the one hand they consider, sometimes with paternalist benevolence, their workers and the general population very intelligent and generally cooperative unless they are stirred up by radical agitators. On the other, they regard the common man as suffering from the legacy of his cultural, historical, and economic shortcomings, and above all, from crucial malnutrition or lack of education with the resulting inertia and irresponsibility.

Investment and Capital Supply

The managers' views of productivity, competition, and market limitations were definitely related to their attitudes toward investment, capital supply, profit, and risk.

In answering the corresponding questions the great majority of interviewees from all the areas covered stated that their enterprises had current intentions to invest more money for expansion or improvement. In some cases it could be established from other sources of information that this intention could not be very serious or realistic, but it was clear that most of the respondents felt something of an economic if not moral obligation to keep investing. Some answered in more or less North American terms that an en-

70

terprise has to grow or die; a few mentioned national development needs as the chief motivation. In most cases, however, investment or expansion was simply taken for granted as an enterprise goal.

There were, to be sure, a number of exceptions from this trend. In some areas of Northeast Brazil, for instance, the prevailing interpretation of expansion appeared to be as something that "happens," not as the result of a conscious investment effort. In various countries interviewees pointed to underemployed existing facilities or to a recent expansion of the firm which thus was felt to need mainly consolidation for some time to come. A few managers, chiefly in the smaller category, thought that they had all the business they could handle or cared to have, that they were getting on in years, or that general conditions were too uncertain for expansion. A merchant in El Salvador said that his firm is stabilized because in a small country like his, it is bad for political, economic, and administrative reasons to be too big. However, such views were those of a small minority even in the countries with least stable conditions.

When asked about the sources of new investment funds, the prevailing answer pointed to heavy reinvestment of profits or to family funds. Often these two things were not clearly distinguished. If the family had many diversified business interests the new investment might come from profits made either in the enterprise concerned or in other business interests of the group. A number of interviewees claimed that not a penny of profit had ever been taken out of the company, for example, because "most of our shareholders are young, active technicians who don't think of immediate yields all the time." (Manager, construction firm, Mexico.) Typically, however, such statements did not allow for substantial salaries which the managers allotted themselves.

Depreciation allowances were rarely mentioned and appeared to be familiar only to a minority. Reliance on new issues of stocks was understandably rare since most of these countries have no really functioning stock market, partly because of the fearful attitude of the small-capital owner. The manager of a bank in Guatemala claimed that its present private stockholders had bought shares from the Government which owned them originally, burned part of them since the enterprise was overcapitalized, then started building up reserves. Banks were mentioned by industrial and commercial managers as a subsidiary source of capital but generally were thought of mainly in terms of commercial day-to-day credit which, for that matter, was mostly thought to be scarce or very expensive.

Foreign sources of capital supply were mentioned only in companies which were partly foreign-owned, were originally foreign creations, or had access to loans from the Export-Import Bank or intergovernmental banks. The possibility of floating bonds abroad or otherwise entering foreign capital markets on a substantial scale was vaguely mentioned by the managers of two companies. It appears, however, to be alien to the thinking of most Latin American enterprise managers at this point. The apparent explanation is that they cannot visualize foreign investors buying their bonds as long as the general atmosphere in that part of the world is seen in Europe and North America as quite unstable. Moreover, few companies feel that they have got sufficient experience or knowledge of foreign capital markets, though some have access to expert financial advice from foreign consultants.

Public sources of private investment at home, on the

other hand, are widely used and generally considered appropriate and necessary. Perhaps the outstanding case is that of the Banco do Nordeste do Brasil. Occasional complaints about red tape and delays were voiced in the area but often seemed to express the lack of acquaintance of the applying firm with the preparation of feasibility studies and systematic expansion projects, and rarely represented a basic attitude of mistrust toward public sources of private capital. On the contrary, there were some expressions of appreciation regarding the "educational" work of the Banco among private firms in initiating them to economic development.

When asked whether there was a shortage of capital in their respective country or area, the great majority answered Yes, although qualifications were frequent. Some interviewees related capital shortage to the difficulty in obtaining equipment on long-term credit abroad. Others said that their own company did not suffer from much shortage because of ample profits, family resources, or foreign contacts, but that a definite shortage of capital did exist in the area. "We always speak of shortage of capital but we always expand. There are many ways to get both capital and credit." (Industrial manager, Mexico.)

A few felt that the apparent shortage of capital for most businesses actually represented wasteful use of the capital available, for example, by buying expensive equipment such as electric office machines without knowing how to use them properly or without utilizing the data accumulated. Such interpretation of capital shortage, however, was fairly rare. An industrial manager in Mexico claimed that the shortage of capital was often created by the industrialist himself through going to the banks instead of reinvesting his profit, the latter being used to go into a *different* business especially if it promised riskless investment. A Venezuelan bank manager claimed that businessmen neither understand fixed assets nor have a real concept of working capital—which, they assume, *must* come from credit.

More frequently the managers pointed to the flight of domestic capital to North America or Europe for reasons of political uncertainty, in particular, and felt that the national or regional capital shortage could be relieved promptly if the private funds invested abroad could be brought back. "If all the Venezuelan money was invested here, *we* could help the United States!" (Commercial manager, Venezuela.) Restrictive government policies and capital waste through inefficient or corrupt public administration were also mentioned. Explanations of capital shortages in industry and commerce as a result of real-estate buying, or else as natural effects of economic growth and widespread construction were offered by others.

Quite often no clear distinction between capital and credit was made. As mentioned earlier, short-term bank credit was considered scarce and expensive by most. However, it was also stated repeatedly that such shortage does not exist for well-managed, firmly rooted enterprises, and that many of the smaller firms do not know how to prepare a good project or to file an acceptable credit application. Quite a number of industrial and commercial managers described their problem as being forced to *give* credit to customers who cannot obtain it from banks, and having frequent difficulty in collecting such advances. However, restrictive attitudes of domestic and foreign banks, especially toward smaller business, were also mentioned.

Finally, effects of a prolonged inflation upon capital supply were repeatedly pointed out in Chile and Brazil. It was felt that capital formation had been rendered extremely difficult, that working capital had actually been eaten up, or that excessive consumption had been encouraged. As is shown in Chapter VI, however, the prevailing attitude toward inflation was ambivalent, interpreting it as evil and beneficial at the same time.

Profit and Risk

The expectation of immediate or prompt profit from new investments was found to prevail in all the countries visited, though the degree or intensity of this expectation varied according to the area and size of the firm. Profit was often related to the gain per unit rather than size of sales. Repeatedly it was added that the expectation of prompt profit remained a pious wish and was at odds with reality much of the time. In the least developed areas the expectation of immediate profit was generally most widespread or there was no perception of any alternative at all.[6] In industrial enterprises, "immediate" usually meant within one year or else after paying back initial loans.

In a few cases, mostly under the influence of foreign executive training or capital participation, there was evidence of expansion planning over several years and readiness to wait for profits to materialize three to five years later. Generally, however, it was felt that under conditions of scanty economic development it was neither necessary to wait for profit nor feasible to do so as long as interest rates were 20 or 30 per cent a year. It was also said repeatedly that small business, at least, could not survive without immediate profit. Curiously enough, this was stressed even in enterprises that had no real cost accounting or inventory

[6] Compare Henry G. Aubrey, "Investment Decisions in Underdeveloped Countries," in *Capital Formation and Economic Growth*, Universities-National Bureau Committee for Economic Research (Princeton, N.J.: Princeton University Press, 1955).

control and thus had no way of calculating their profit accurately.

As for risk-taking, the response, with few exceptions, was clear-cut, and of a nature that may surprise readers from more developed areas. The interviewees typically did not think of either business or expansion in terms of risk. The latter is something to be avoided; when there is risk there will be no new investment. Risk might be all right for companies in wealthy countries, but in the poorer areas nobody could afford it. On the basis of this general mentality the usual answer was that there was no risk in producing brands already known, that the consuming population was eagerly awaiting new products or supplies so that no risk was involved in expansion, or that the market situation had carefully been explored first and that management had come to the conclusion that *no* risk was involved in the expansion contemplated save for unforeseeable political, monetary, or international hazards. In current transactions the collection of debts from customers was classified by some as risky in an unwanted way.

Certainly this attitude is a far cry from the Schumpeterian entrepreneur whom some contemporary writers consider the mainstay of coming economic development in less developed areas today, more or less on the lines of Western Europe in the eighteenth and nineteenth centuries. (See Chapter VIII.) Paradoxically, excessive risk-taking of a noncalculated type, pursued as a get-rich-quick or Easy Street device, is quite frequent, but real perception of calculated-risk ventures as the essence or even as a substantial part of business activity is much rarer. Exceptions are presented by a few businessmen who deal in commodities whose supply inevitably fluctuates a great deal according to weather conditions or mineral deposits found, and by executives of a few companies who have been strongly influenced by North American or Western European training or capital participation.

Some examples of productive calculated risk-taking can be found, however. The head of a Mexican company which had started out selling imported goods and then shifted to industrial production on an ever more diversified scale remarked, "After the Second World War we became aware of the industrial development of Mexico, and lived it!"

In summary, the understanding of productivity is limited and the function of management in promoting it even more so. This limitation affects the efficient implementation of the widespread drive for expansion and investment—a drive that is based on a certain sense of obligation which, however, is rarely associated directly or definitely with national development needs. The prevailing sources of capital regarded as available are reinvested profits, family funds, and public loan institutions. Shortage of capital is perceived as quite grave but this perception is modified by reference to capital invested abroad or wasted, or to inflation effects. Expectation of immediate profit from new investments prevails, and risk is mostly seen as a hazard that must and can be avoided.

Since competition, market limitations, productivity trends, and the supply of capital and credit are viewed at best with moderate optimism and at worst with fatalistic inertia, it will be interesting to relate these attitudes to those concerning the economic development stage achieved, the measures needed, and the stimuli expected to be given to both enterprise and development from *external* sources, namely, the government and the outside world. Attitudes toward these two factors will be examined in the two chapters that follow.

VI

Government and Development

HOW did the rather vivid if not always clear views of market, production, and investment problems facing the managers' own firms compare with their thinking on the national development process and the public role in it? This comparison was the object of the questions, "Do you think this country in general is well on its way to full economic development or not?" and "What do you think is needed most badly in order to stimulate economic development?"

A considerable variety of answers was received, not only in relation to the developmental stage of the country and region concerned but also according to the age group, managerial background, education, and personality of the respondent. There was much uncertainty and confusion on the part of the smaller, older, less educated, and more isolated businessmen who had not really thought before in these terms or in those of the national economy in general.

Development Stage Achieved

An understandable response of many was that development of their country was in progress but still had a long way to go, or that development was not fast enough in relation to the legacy of the past or to the recent population pressure. Similarly some others classified the present stage as the mere beginning of development, the main reason given being that the common people get little out of it as yet. A substantial group, especially in countries like Guatemala and Peru but including several others, even some with sizable industries, felt in effect that their country was still distinctly underdeveloped, though this word was not especially popular because of its possible noneconomic connotations.

Compared with other countries, this one is still underdeveloped since nearly all its income depends on agriculture. There has been some industrialization but not on the basis of its own raw materials. We have chiefly assembly industries. Moreover, income per head is very low, there is complete lack of education among the Indians, and 60 per cent of the people produce practically nothing. They need to be educated not only in reading and writing but in producing. A total transformation of the culture is required. There is no definite plan for economic growth; private enterprise has tried to grow as best it could but lags behind population growth. The trouble with this country is that it is too rich by nature, so that few people do any real work. We need diversification of agriculture and of the entire economy, but without *economía dirigida*. (Agricultural manager, Guatemala.)

Everywhere, even including Argentina, managerial thinking emphasized the substantial continuing development needs of the country. This was stressed not only in the North American sense of never standing still but in the sense of an urgent and decisive need to amplify industrial facilities, raise agricultural productivity, and secure modern housing, education, and health facilities for the general population. In Chile, reinterviews in 1963 showed wide dissatisfaction with the pace of development during the intervening period, with the possible exception of roads and housing.

On the other hand, an industrial manager in Mexico claimed that "Mexico is the least stupid of the Latin American countries and is growing much faster than the others, with a minimum of planning." Some others thought that Mexico was not an underdeveloped country any longer or that it was definitely heading for full development. But a number of interviewees felt that Mexico was still deeply underdeveloped and that much of the industrial growth consisted of unhealthy, expensive hothouse industries.

Sometimes development was related to business fluctuations:

Comparatively, this country is the one-eyed in the realm of the blind. In absolute terms, we had a fictitious boom after the war, then a slump which brought us back to our senses, and now development is far more solid. Enterprises plan better now; the good ones survived and are growing. (Industrialist, Venezuela.)

Qualified statements concerning the current stage of economic development were frequent, for example, in commenting that in some respects it was well on its way while in others it was not, or in regarding "underdevelopment" a misleading term altogether. A Mexican banker and promoter defined underdevelopment as an imbalance

Government and Development

among the sectors of the economy insofar as the relative demand originating in them is concerned. Agriculture, education, housing, and in some cases communications or water and power supply were seen as laggards behind a relatively advanced condition of industry, mining, and commercial construction. "Infrastructure" had clearly become one of the most popular and perhaps most misused words in economic conversations in Latin America.

What *is* the borderline of "development"? Generally this country still requires enormous activities for development. It needs new investments in line with the population increase, better education, infrastructure, aid to the neglected regions. All the sectors are interdependent and a coordinated plan is needed including both agriculture and industry, capital goods and mechanization, employment, housing, and so forth. (Manager, financial company, Mexico.)

Venezuela today is like a teen-ager who can already use his father's shoes but not yet his pants. There has been *uncoordinated* growth, for historical reasons. Independence cost more lives here than anywhere else in Latin America. There followed a sequence of personal regimes of various dictators, and each time the opposition and the intellectuals wound up in jail or in exile. Gómez and his successors brought haphazard industries, with far-reaching lack of managerial and intellectual organization. These are the roots of our present stage. (Industrial manager, Venezuela.)

Regional differences in the stage of economic development within the country were often pointed out. Such feelings are understandably strong in Brazil, not only in the poverty-stricken Northeast but in the more developed South. However, a Northeastern interviewee felt that there really are *three* Northeasts, and that compared with Pernambuco or Bahia his own state of Ceará represents the forgotten area. Thinking of São Paulo in all the parts visited of the Northeast was frequently found to be in terms of a "foreign," wealthy, perhaps imperialist nation.

I am so involved in this company that I study little about Brazil in general. But all the Presidents have been Southerners and political considerations have dominated the economic policy of the nation. The North has practically been abandoned, especially Bahia. And in local decisions concerning roads, for instance, political yardsticks also prevail. The State Government mostly knows what is right but does not do it. Too many things are done as favors to friends, even when economically useless. (Industrial manager, Bahia, Northeast Brazil.)

The "country of the future" phase is still used as an excuse. Brazil as a whole is well on its way to maturity, despite its people, but the Northeast still depends on politics. Either it solves its problem by providing jobs in unorthodox ways or it will blow up. The Northeast is like a country of its own, but the sugar kings don't see the times and the needs. This area is not so much underdeveloped as undertreated. It could be another São Paulo. (Industrial manager, Northeast Brazil, European-born.)

"Exports" mean in the Northeast not only sales to the United States or Great Britain but to Guanabara or Minas Gerais as well. Even in the much smaller Chile, for that matter, managerial thinking in such areas as Osorno and Puerto Montt was found to be focused in a large degree on regional, rather than national, underdevelopment.

Political preconditions of, or obstacles to, fuller economic development were often cited in response to the question mentioned, as will be shown later in some detail. It was said, for example, that the country concerned *could* be well on its way to full development if it were not for the vagaries of politics, governmental indecision, red tape, encroachment upon private enterprise, or corruption and theft of national funds. Others said in a somewhat similar vein that development would be in full swing if it were not for Communist or radical propaganda, unrest, or violence.

However, affirmative aspects of governmental development activities, such as public financing of private enterprise, were also mentioned frequently. In Mexico, pride about the Revolution and the reconstruction of economic and social thinking it had brought about was mixed with misgivings about a political and agrarian degeneration of the Revolution in recent years. Statements about the interdependence and the necessity of parallel development of agriculture and industry were also frequent in Mexico.[1]

Development Role of Private Enterprise

As for the role of private enterprise itself in the economic development of the nation concerned, we have mentioned already that any positive perception of this role as a dynamic factor was confined to a distinct minority of the interviewees and in some areas to a few persons only.

Many businessmen are not especially satisfied with economic development thus far. Now they must really work in order to survive in the market! So they complain, even though they are not enemies of the development idea. (Bank manager, Mexico.)

In most of the areas visited the manager or businessman who thought of himself or his firm in general terms of entrepreneurship or a pioneering role in economic development had remained a fairly rare bird. Economic development received much lip service, but it was something

[1] Compare Raymond Vernon, *The Dilemma of Mexico's Development* (Cambridge, Mass.: Harvard University Press, 1963), especially Chap. 6.

that seemed to happen independently of business decisions, though simultaneously with them. It was something for which "they"—the Government, the development planners, perhaps the foreign aid agencies or objective changes in the world markets—were responsible, not "we" in the sense of enterprise managers as individuals or as a group.

Such restraint could reflect the institutional and social changes of the last four decades,[2] and it might be healthy insofar as it had prevented excessive dreams of social leadership on the part of the business groups, such as existed in some other parts of the world. However, it had also remained an impediment to specific perceptions of the need for active participation in the national development process on the part of every major group of society. Even in São Paulo, probably the most advanced area of industrialization in Latin America, a United Nations study came to the following conclusion:

It can be ventured to state that the major part of industrialists hold a false idea of the economic development process in which they are involved and to which they contribute in practice. In reality, the social conditions of the formation of an industrial bourgeoisie in São Paulo have had the effect that many industrialists do not notice that they are the principal beneficiaries of the development of a domestic market and that

---

[2] "The era of the Schumpeterian innovator has passed for Latin America. Economic development can no longer be left to the impulses of the entrepreneur, the public official, or the empirical politician. It must be fully recognized that growth cannot be accelerated unless the educational system and the existing social organizations—trade unions, producer associations, public agencies, and others—train in both the private and the public sectors the professional managerial elements who will assume responsibility and make the decisions necessary for economic progress." Victor L. Urquidi, *The Challenge of Development in Latin America* (New York: Frederick A. Praeger, Inc., 1964), pp. 82ff.

they derive advantages from the processes that promote it even when such processes may present different and negative aspects to other social groups.[3]

An exception to such perceptual limitations was supplied by an industrial manager with academic background in Chile (reinterview 1963) who commented that the real problem was how to make the private sector parallel public investment.

The Government does not understand this problem and concentrates on public finance. Private business must organize itself, too, in order to understand the Government's problem and to take an active part in the development program through appropriate investments in the private sector.

Another kind of exception was provided, up to a point, by a four-day meeting of most of the leading Venezuelan businessmen on the social responsibilities of private enterprise, held in Maracay in February 1963.[4] Even on this

[3] Naciones Unidas, Comisión Económica para América Latina, *El Empresario Industrial en América Latina*, Part 2 (Brazil) (Santiago, Chile: 1963), mimeo., p. 66. (Other parts of this interview study deal with Argentina, Chile, and Colombia.) Compare the following statement from Eugenio Heiremans D., President of the Sociedad de Fomento Fabril in Chile, "In formulating national development plans, private enterprise can adopt no other attitude than to cooperate diligently in the preliminary study and implementation of such plans."—Inter-American Development Bank, *Private Enterprise and Latin American Development* (Washington, D.C.: Inter-American Development Bank, 1962), p. 6. Also Chandulal N. Vakil, "Business Leadership in Underdeveloped Countries," *Industrialization and Productivity*, United Nations Bulletin No. 2 (1959). For a discussion of some related motivational and behavioral characteristics of entrepreneurs and managers in less developed countries, David C. McClelland, *The Achieving Society* (Princeton, N.J.: D. Van Nostrand Company, Inc., 1961), Chaps. 6–7.

[4] See various mimeographed materials of the Asociación Venezolana de Ejecutivos, Caracas, 1963, including a summary by Ivan

occasion, however, emphasis was placed mainly on the contribution of private enterprise to education, low-cost housing, and health facilities for workers, rather than on active private cooperation in national development planning. Some speakers felt that the first social responsibility of private enterprise consisted in producing, thus achieving profit. An earlier, much-discussed document from business sources on economic development, known as *Carta Económica de Mérida* (Federación Venezolana de Cámaras y Asociaciones de Comercio y Producción, Caracas, 1962) had confined itself mainly to pointing out the necessity of a definite development policy in general.

Development Measures Needed

What were the greatest needs of the various countries assumed to be at this juncture in order to create stronger stimuli to economic development? A great variety of responses to this question were received even within each area. The most frequent answers can be grouped as follows:

(a) *Good government.* It was interesting to find the answer to an economic question presented with much frequency in *political* terms, especially as this occurred all over Latin America. The specific content of this kind of answer ranged all the way from emotional charges of radicalism or corruption in the government to the detached

Lansberg Henríquez under the title *Una Nueva Actitud* (A New Attitude). Reprinted in *La Responsabilidad Empresarial en el Desarrollo Social de Venezuela* (Caracas: Asociación Venezolana de Ejecutivos, 1963). Also Luis Vallenilla, *The Distribution of Opportunity in Venezuela* (Caracas: Asociación Venezolana de Ejecutivos, 1963). Consejo Interamericano Económico y Social, *Desarrollo Industrial y Financiamento del Sector Privado,* São Paulo meeting, 1963, mimeo.

discussion of cumbersome import licenses or tax procedures, to incompetence of many public administrators
despite well-meaning intentions, or to the inner workings
of the political party in power, but the basic approach was
similar in each case.[5] The number-one stimulus to fuller
economic development was usually considered to be "confidence" based on a better political system with greater
stability and more clearly defined goals.

What we need most urgently is a political system that would
resolve the socialist, statist, and fascist tendencies in our economic development including pressure-group influences from
cotton or meat producers, for instance. We need a third position.
Mexico is not a capitalist country because there is no private
initiative, just protectionism. On the other hand, the socialist
tendencies here are not Marxist. The real danger is fascism à la
Spain. Mexico needs to define its development in a way which is
neither socialist nor fascist. "Revolution" is quite insufficient,
and Rostow's "stages" don't help us much either. Thus far all
the development planning has been in government hands, private
enterprise has not contributed to it though it should. They
should say what *they* will contribute to development! But the
employers' groups have no positive plan and no research departments. (Manager, public enterprise, Mexico.)

We are still in the underdeveloped category and shall be for
many years. There is no continuity in government with regard
to economic development. They only speak of it in an abstract
way, don't know what to emphasize and what to do. (Industrial
manager, El Salvador.)

[5] Professor Hirschman points to the possible energizing function
of the dissatisfaction both of entrepreneurs and policy-makers with
past governmental policies. See Albert O. Hirschman, *Journeys
toward Progress: Studies of Economic Policy-Making in Latin
America* (New York: Twentieth Century Fund, 1963), pp. 244ff.

(b) *Education.* In this case, too, the answer to the economic question asked was at first glance, at least, non-economic. Education was seen as the fundamental need in the interest of *economic* development by numerous managers all the way from the Rio Grande to the Tierra del Fuego.

Economic development must be rooted in cultural development. High incomes without education do not result in proper use of the increased resources. We need extensive rural education, not only the three R's but hygiene, better living, better land use, production techniques. The land is fertile here, but people eat watery fruits with little nutritive value. They produce them on much land and keep eating them, even though vegetables would be much better for them. Cooperatives for production and distribution are also needed. (Manager, industrial and agricultural enterprise, El Salvador.)

There were some responses to the contrary, to be sure. Some skepticism or fear of dangerous thoughts was voiced toward the education of *indígenas,* rural laborers, or urban slum dwellers. Some qualifications were also made concerning the kind of education most badly needed; for example, priority for technical instruction or for secondary schools. But such occasional reservations were far outweighed by the stress which a number of enterprise managers put on education in general and, with it, on the rise of a new generation as the most important precondition for effective economic development. "Education is an investment with an extremely high yield, economically and otherwise." (Industrialist, Venezuela.)

(c) *Agrarian reform.* Great regional as well as substantive differences were encountered in this respect. To begin with, spontaneous mention by managers of reforms or changes badly needed in the agrarian structure or policy of their country was very frequent in some areas, such as Mexico, and infrequent in others such as Chile, especially during the original interviews there in 1959–1960. Even more important, the kind of measures required was interpreted in very different ways. In Northeast Brazil much "hydraulic thinking" in the sense of an interpretation of that region's development lag in terms of deficient water supply and storage, rather than in terms of a backward socioeconomic structure, was still encountered. Of those who mentioned the need for agrarian changes there (many did not) some thought mainly of building more reservoirs and pipelines in order to reduce the irregularity of water supply in the *sertão* or dry hinterland. In Mexico, which had started its agrarian revolution over half a century ago, managers criticized chiefly slowness, inefficiency, credit abuses, or political favoritism in the *ejido* system. Many recommended a transition to full peasant ownership of the land and an end to new, illegal concentration of land in the hands of politicians.

In both of the areas mentioned and in various others there was frequent emphasis on the need for efficient size of farms, rural mechanization and credit, utilization of unused land, prevention of erosion, water supply, education, and cooperative organization. The most widespread agreement, including areas where agrarian changes were rarely mentioned spontaneously as urgent need, consisted in emphasis on including the rural masses into the national market of which they are not yet part today. This was often regarded as an essential condition of industrialization as well.

Rural education and housing are decisive; without them there can be no real consumption. The agrarian problem is very complex. My family has suffered from the reforms, but I think they are in order if they lead to higher consumption and individual property rights, not just to political influence in agriculture. (Industrial manager, Mexico.)

(d) *Industrialization.* Interestingly, only a minority of interviewees, even those in manufacturing, spontaneously mentioned industrialization as the most urgent aspect of economic development. The apparent reason has been indicated already. With the exception of major industrial concentrations already in existence, such as São Paulo or Buenos Aires, some aspect of the "infrastructure"— whether education, roads, sanitation, or some other need— or else the creation of a larger consumer market out of the poverty-stricken, ignorant *rural* masses was considered by many managers interviewed an indispensable setting for substantial industrial development, which would also absorb rural excess manpower. Given such a setting, indeed, the belief in developmental emphasis on extensive industries was quite widespread both among manufacturers and among other businessmen. This also applied to more general views on the need for diversification of the respective national production.

The importance of small and medium-sized industrial plants in rural areas, even when the production costs of such plants are somewhat higher than those of larger units, was pointed out repeatedly. So was the need for ample and cheap supply of credit and capital for industrial purposes, but there were some warnings against excessive mechanization which a poor country with small markets could not afford.

Industrial orientation toward foreign markets, on the other hand, appeared to be rare at the time of the interviews. Few were the industrial managers in Latin America, even in Brazil, who were thinking seriously about the prospects of a successful competition abroad including other parts of Latin America. This hesitation restricted considerably managerial thinking about the possibilities of a Latin American Common Market (to be discussed in Chapter VII) with the notable exception of the more limited Central American Common Market which had entered distinctly into the consideration of many managers interviewed in Guatemala and El Salvador. One of them commented:

This is a moment of *incipient* industrial development, of transformation away from an agricultural economy. Agriculture will always remain essential here, but in a more mechanized form and this applies to coffee, too. Only the efficient agricultural enterprises will survive, and agriculture will be reduced to an economically feasible extent. The bulk of the working force will go into industry, though the latter must remain somewhat limited here. (Manager of industrial and agricultural enterprise, El Salvador.)

(e) *Monetary stability.* This need was mentioned by many interviewees in Chile and Brazil, but even in these countries with their long history of monetary instability some other need appeared to a number of interviewees as more urgent. In other areas, such as Argentina, the question of monetary stabilization was seen by many primarily as one aspect of the more general problem of political stability. But in Venezuela, where political conditions were very much on the mind of nearly every interviewee, spontaneous mention of monetary stability as principal requirement was rare. One commercial manager there, however, was emphatic in claiming that there was a hidden inflation which was of no benefit to commerce as demand was inelastic, meaning that the income of the rank and file was lagging and did not permit advance purchases in anticipation of rising prices. In Mexico monetary instability was usually referred to only as a thing of the pre-

1954 past. In other words, vivid recollection of monetary
instability and the emphasis on monetary stabilization as the
chief requirement of development policy did not appear to
have survived longer than for a few years the actual conspicuous condition of unstable money.

It is interesting to note that foreign aid and investment
were rarely mentioned as the principal requirement for
successful development even though the overwhelming
majority of interviewees in most countries thought of both
as a continuing need of their economies in a *complementary* sense. In every country the questions about the stage
of economic development and the measures needed were
answered almost invariably in terms of some kind of domestic requirement. Only in those cases where the interviewee was under the erroneous impression that the
interviewer was connected with aid-granting agencies
abroad was a casual or joking hint made that the country
needed a lot of dollars. There was no evidence anywhere,
least of all in the large countries, of real or basic reliance on
foreign development aid. This would seem to be at odds
with widespread preconceptions in the United States according to which nearly everybody in Latin America
either thinks or claims that he depends on U.S. funds for
further development.

The prevailing managerial thinking encountered thus
perceived the economic stage of the country in question as
incipient development, with regional differentiation and
frequent qualifications including some of a political nature.
There was little interpretation of private entrepreneurship
as the real spark in economic development. Among the
greatest needs in developing the country concerned, good
government, education, agrarian changes, industrialization,
and monetary stability were mentioned most frequently,

Government and Development

while foreign aid and investment were usually considered a complementary but not a decisive need. This latter aspect will be discussed in the next chapter. First, however, we need to examine the managerial views of the relationship between development needs, inflationary influences, and the general role of government in economic development.

Inflation and Development

With great national variations, the prevailing managerial attitude toward inflation was found to be rather ambivalent. On the one hand, inflation was seen as a scourge which made reliable calculation, long-range planning, and the accumulation or preservation of working capital next to impossible, fostered speculative misuse of funds, made the consumer buy in excess of his real needs, favored the debtor, and forced labor into a constant vain fight for the preservation of its already low standard of living. Such criticism was sometimes focused on nondevelopmental (for example, military) roots or forms of inflation.

On the other hand, inflation was also seen as generating a continuous business boom, and, more important, as inevitable basis or consequence of economic development. A Brazilian industrialist assured me in 1960 that no one had ever asked him before whether development might not be possible without inflation. At times it was claimed that inflation would end *after* development was achieved, just like a millionnaire getting respectable once he has made his fortune.

The emphasis on the favorable or the unfavorable aspects of inflation varied according to the country and individual, but some combination of both aspects in the mind of the same person was frequent. Inflation was rarely interpreted as the unmixed, devilish evil as which it is usually seen by enterprise managers in more advanced countries. It was usually considered desirable to keep down the annual rate of inflation to a moderate level. But it was also felt that textbook concepts of sound money do not really apply to countries with vast unexploited resources assuming only that the population tends to plow inflationary gains right back into increased production, not into speculation or luxuries. An Argentine industrialist said, "People are *born* either inflationists or deflationalists, and the group I belong to has an inflationary bias because we feel that there is no economic development without inflation."

In the detailed investigation of managerial attitudes in Chile, which was carried out in 1959–1960, interviewees had been asked in a somewhat different vein whether any lasting effects of the prolonged inflationary history of that country upon the mentality of the people were likely to continue even into a new period of stabilization. At the time mentioned Chile seemed to have entered such a period, though this appearance was not borne out by subsequent events. About one-half of those with opinions thought at the time that psychological effects of the long inflation would persist despite stabilization.

During the later phases of the investigation important variations in the prevailing responses were encountered according to the monetary history of the country concerned as well as the monetary situation during the period immediately preceding the interview. In Guatemala it was repeatedly pointed out (during the summer of 1962) that although the country had grave economic problems inflation was not one of them. In Mexico inflation was mostly referred to as a thing of the past. However, some respondents were not certain whether the danger had passed for good, pointed to many people's preference for dollar holdings, stressed the continuing if slow rise in wages and prices that was still going on under the surface of monetary stability, or felt uneasy about the slowed-down rate of economic growth.

One Mexican interviewee claimed that business there *produces* inflation by raising prices without any economic reason. Another said that Mexico had a cost inflation but no monetary inflation, and still others defined inflation not as a monetary problem but one of stagnating production or poor market organization. A banker in El Salvador, on the other hand, feared that foreign loans might have an inflationary effect since some of them were not productive, and that they might also impair domestic initiative and the "art of thinking."

In none of the countries that had *not* experienced a sweeping inflation in recent years could any belief be found among managers that extensive inflation was required or inevitable in order to develop the economy of the country. Some references were made, especially in Mexico, to the dangers of *deflation* or else to harmful restrictions on private credit in favor of public investment.

Right now we are having an incredible recession in construction, for instance. The government does not pay the constructors and they, in turn, owe us money. Public works don't make up for this. We have a deflation problem. (Industrial manager, Mexico.)

No country ever passes over this phase, but in the light of the last ten years we have no inflation now. Money and prices are stabilized, real wages have gone up. But this stabilization has braked the development of the country and should perhaps be undone. The problem is how to do it in a controlled way. It's like getting "a little pregnant." The rich favor inflation as it brings them real-estate gains. (Commercial manager, Mexico.)

A Mexican banker with academic background claimed that all the public investment has inflationary tendencies but that it is necessary just the same in order to provide the infrastructure for private enterprise and to supplement the latter. He referred to himself as a Keynesian with a dynamic approach.

In Brazil, on the other hand, the interviews held in 1960 in the Southern, relatively developed parts of the country such as Rio Grande do Sul, São Paulo, and Minas Gerais showed a frequent association, even identification, in the minds both of enterprise managers and economists of inflation with economic development. In other words, inflation was merely seen as one aspect of development, and the latter could not be imagined without the former.[6]

During the second round of interviews in Brazil, in early 1963, a different atmosphere was encountered, though we must allow for the fact that this second round was held chiefly in the far less developed Northeast. Conceivably the geographic, historical, and developmental difference might be reflected in the responses received. At any rate, criticism among enterprise managers of the sweeping inflation of the preceding year or two was very widespread. Some of them rated comparative stabilization of exchange rates and prices as the most urgent requirement. On the other hand, there was much concern about the effects of a deflation, too. Nearly everyone of the critics added that *some* inflation was inevitable in the course of economic development, especially industrialization, but that it should be controlled and kept down to a maximum of perhaps 12 or 15 per cent

[6] Compare Werner Baer, "Brazil: Inflation and Economic Efficiency," *Economic Development and Cultural Change* (July, 1963), especially pp. 404ff.

a year. A mining manager in Central Brazil commented in 1963:

The history of Brazilian inflation and development is very complicated. Higher urbanization has brought an increase of the money economy but also of productivity. This is not a "closed economy"; it is an expanding economy, geographically and otherwise. It is confidence in the future that determines the actual effects of inflation. Industry feels that this is the main stimulus to them in producing profits which, in this country, are largely reinvested. Brazil has had no other experience. People are used to inflation and behave accordingly. Profits have not decreased here, though depreciation allowances can only be calculated on a historical basis which may be very deceptive.

There is far more concern, however, about the rate of inflation. Brasilia has increased the inflation, but this increase has been marginal and it has given some development to the State of Goiás. But anything that is being done with inflation could also be done without it, though inflation *is* compatible with economic growth.

A commercial manager in Northeast Brazil stated:

Inflation has been favorable for us in general as our export earnings have grown in local currency terms. Retail business is financed with other people's money. For the country, inflation has also been helpful in that it has accelerated the disintegration of outmoded social institutions and has speeded up changes in the old patterns of prestige and power. However, inflation is now more a political than an economic problem. The government has the power to stop it, but this would require careful analysis of the economic effects of a stabilization.

In a somewhat comparable vein, the original optimism of a sizable segment of business managers in Chile concerning a durable stabilization had suffered severely by the time of the reinterviews held in early 1963.

What bothers the businessman here is not that he does not make money—he does—but that he is working and saving for nothing, unless he invests his profits abroad. That's just what I have been doing. (Merchant, Chile, reinterview, 1963.)

Wages have been rising much faster than productivity, for political reasons, and so has the cost of government. Make me a dictator and I'll solve the inflation problem immediately. (Industrial manager, Chile, reinterview, 1963.)

In Mexico, an industrial manager said:

In all of Latin America there are always inflationary tendencies but this is like medicine: Too much is harmful while a small dose heals. However, autosuggestion is possible here. Government economists should tell us how to avoid inflation but also stagnation. I think the Brazilians are *locos*.

Similarly, the manager of an industrial and agricultural enterprise in El Salvador asked:

If it were possible to have a controlled inflation, this could be a very good stimulus to consumption and production. But can it be done?

A fact of considerable importance which emerged from the interviews nearly everywhere was that inflation more often than not was equated with unstable exchange rates, especially a rising rate of the dollar. This interpretation can partly be explained from the basic importance of foreign trade for the economy of every Latin American country, especially the necessity to import many industrial products including equipment for development projects. However, the association mentioned went beyond that. Inflation appeared to be regarded by many as a *result* of a weak

Government and Development

exchange rate of the domestic currency—due to lagging exports, unfavorable terms of trade, speculation, or political unrest—not as a cause of such weakness. At the same time, rise in the domestic price level was widely considered an unavoidable result of monetary weakness given the significance of imported goods on the national markets. At the time of the reinterviews in Chile in early 1963 such inflationary expectations were widely associated with the devaluation of the *escudo* at the end of 1961, even though actual price increases had remained moderate.

Specific association of inflation with the domestic flow of money, budget deficits, credit policy, investment, employment, consumption and savings trends was limited to a distinct minority of the managers interviewed. Some, it is true, pointed to consumer habits formed in the past, political pressures, population increase, or growth of the economy in general as factors which, to their mind, made some degree of inflation inevitable. But real understanding of the relationship between inflation and the general economic situation and policy was not found to be very frequent. On the other hand, inflation was widely associated with shortage of credit and high interest rates, though it was not always recognized that the latter might be negative on the real level; that is, when they lagged behind the rate of inflation. The eroding effect of inflation upon the working capital of firms was widely stressed.

Other adverse aspects of inflation that preoccupied the managers were "speculation," especially protective buying of real estate and hard currencies; capital flight which was not ordinarily seen as foreign investment in reverse but as the real cause of the much-discussed capital shortage at home, this shortage thus being interpreted in part as a result of actual or feared inflation; lagging incentives to step up efficiency of production; and the interplay between bad money and bad government. The politicians, in the view of some interviewees in various countries, were using the abundance of new money spent by the government, or their advance knowledge of devaluation measures, in order to fill their own pockets.

To restate the findings in this field, enterprise managers tended to consider inflation either damaging altogether or somewhat beneficial to their own companies in the short run, but adverse in the long run, especially when the rate of price increases or currency depreciation exceeded something like 15 per cent a year. They were in general more inclined to regard a controlled, moderate inflation—as opposed to a restrictive deflation policy which a good many of them associated with the International Monetary Fund —as beneficial or, at least, inevitable from the viewpoint of national economic development. They were far more prone to associate inflation with upward changes in the value of foreign currencies than with the general economic condition and policy of their own country. And they were subject to psychological influences rooted both in the length and intensity of inflation experiences in their own country and in the monetary happenings there during the preceding few years.

Inability of a government to prevent inflation, or a conscious inflationary policy, were thus interpreted by many managers as influences that had some favorable along with many unfavorable aspects. At any rate, they felt that they had to live with such influences somehow for the foreseeable future as they had in the past.

Positive Development Role of the State

In relation to perceived development needs and possible inflationary expectations, how was the development role of the state interpreted in a more general sense? As was pointed out earlier, the structure and investment facilities of many enterprises in Latin America are not yet geared effectively to economic development. Since many enterprise managers turned out to be aware of this limitation, to what extent did they expect the state to take over the development task and to fill the gap left by private enterprise?

In North America and parts of Western Europe emotional or dogmatic approaches to the problem of government activity in economic life have long prevailed among private businessmen even at times when decisive public offices have been run by experienced managers freshly out of corporation offices. The underlying belief has been that government can never do any good in economic life and that it is always bound to be inefficient no matter who runs it. The psychological roots of this attitude, especially the status jealousy involved, have been discussed elsewhere.[7]

Such abstract hostility toward governmental intervention, it is true, has seldom been implemented in the daily practice of private firms in their relations with government agencies or in their use of public facilities. Tariffs, subsidies, credit guarantees, defense contracts, and numerous other measures of government intervention have been readily accepted and actively sought. But an almost schizophrenic cleavage between this practice and the abstract principles has persisted, especially in the United States.

How does this cleavage compare with managerial attitudes toward the government in less developed areas, in this case Latin America, both on the abstract and practical levels? Is an earlier stage of economic development, and the prevalence of urgent needs for developmental stimulation

[7] Albert Lauterbach, *Man, Motives, and Money,* 2nd ed., (Ithaca, N.Y.: Cornell University Press, 1959), pp. 73ff.

conducive to different attitudes? How does private enterprise view its own function in the public development effort? These questions were explored in the interviews with considerable variety of results.[8] Generally speaking, the greatest approximation to the prevailing mentality of North American managers was found in Venezuela where the direct and indirect influence of business ideology and specific business groups from the United States is especially strong.

The attitudes encountered in the various countries of Latin America toward government activity had several aspects.

1. *State enterprises* were generally looked upon with little favor but this view was seldom expressed in a dogmatic vein. The most frequent statement of an adverse nature referred to those state enterprises that competed with private companies, especially when this was practiced under unequal conditions. State monopolies of a complementary nature in fields where private enterprise, under the conditions of the country concerned, was not considered to be applicable—for example, where it had failed earlier or where especially great capital requirements or non-economic factors of importance were present—found relatively little criticism of a general character.

Private initiative has often shown too little push. Some industries are not entered into by private enterprises, therefore, the government *must* intervene. There is no point in protesting against it and then accepting the money. Ideally the government should not be in industry, but this is only abstract. (Bank manager, Mexico.)

[8] The questions concerned were: (a) "What do you think is the most pressing need of this country in order to stimulate development?" (b) "What do you consider the proper role of the state in economic development?"

Some managers thought, however, that even a justified entry of the state into industry should only be temporary and that such enterprises should eventually be turned over to private management.

On the other hand, the actual conduct or efficiency level of public enterprise management, present or past, was often criticized, with the exception of some major CORFO (Corporación de Fomento de la Producción) enterprises in Chile. Entry of state enterprises into fields where private business was already active, excessive draining-off of scarce capital resources at the expense of private enterprise, political yardsticks in management, and nationalization of existing private firms were universally rejected. But complementary action of the state in fields which private enterprise could not cover (for example, communications, irrigation, or low-cost housing) was widely approved. A private real-estate man in Mexico showed to a visitor with pride a public housing development which he considered necessary as private enterprise could not build good dwellings for the poor at reasonable rents.

"Nationalization" in the sense of the nation taking over foreign holdings in *basic*, especially extractive, industries such as oil found relatively little resistance. PEMEX (Petróleos Mexicanos) despite some criticism of its management practice was, at least, accepted as an established political-historical fact by the great majority of interviewees in Mexico and very few suggested that it be denationalized. This prevailing acceptance also applied to public transportation services everywhere. One private manager said, though, that PEMEX represents a very special case: it exploits natural wealth and can thus afford to do the wrong things, but the state fails when faced with international competition. Another interviewee characterized PEMEX as a "public service" but added, in line with many others, that petrochemical production should be private.

An industrial manager in Venezuela felt that oil production there could not be owned by domestic private capital, while another one felt equally strongly that oil should not be administered by the state in any form.[9] As for petrochemicals, controlled private management was preferred by most managers in that country, too. There seemed to be little hostility toward the state-owned autonomous Corporación Venezolana de Guyana, a steel-coal-power-community planning complex, and its cooperation with private foreign enterprises was widely approved.

In other words, criticism of state enterprise was focused, first, on fields where private initiative was active and more or less successful and, second, on inadequate management practices and political influences even where public ownership as such was not necessarily considered unacceptable for a limited period, at least. On the other hand, managers of public enterprise stressed the frequent necessity of keeping their prices low even when they were in a monopolistic position, of letting their wage costs rise even when there was no economic justification for such a policy, and of avoiding spending in hard currencies even when preference for domestic or soft-currency goods involved a financial loss.

2. *Infrastructure* was the focus of the other attitudinal extreme on the part of enterprise managers. It also was a concept used rather loosely by a number of them. The idea that the government should provide certain preconditions

[9] Encuesta, C. A., in Caracas, published in early 1963 a study, *Imagen Pública de la Empresa Privada*, which, admittedly on the basis of a very limited sample, showed 74 per cent of those questioned (81 per cent in the low-income group) as favoring the nationalization of the petroleum industry.

of business activity and economic development, and that without such action no development would be possible, especially in industry, was found to be very widespread in all the countries visited.

The definition of infrastructure, however, varied a great deal. In some areas the accent was put on roads, transportation and communications in general, water supply, power facilities, or land reclamation. Elsewhere there was greater emphasis on public health, judicial administration and, especially, education.

This country needs education first, *then* democracy, otherwise communism will come along with democracy. (Merchant, El Salvador.)

Housing the poor, both in rural areas and in mushrooming urban or suburban areas, was considered by many interviewees to be a legitimate task for the government. In El Salvador, for example, many interviewees classified housing as its most urgent task. The need to provide job opportunities was stressed in this connection.

The present Government is doing what a democratic government should do: be interested in the people, offer social security, hospitals, and education to workers and peasants. Criticism of this as "socialism" misses the point. These measures have a direct effect on business by increasing the consumption. (Industrial manager, Mexico.)

Laissez-faire is an error; I am for social liberalism. But the state should not compete with private enterprise. (President, employers' group, Mexico.)

3. *Aid to private enterprise*, too, was predominantly accepted as a legitimate and necessary field of public activity if not a "right" of private enterprise. Especially was such aid to be supplied through technical assistance, re-

search, and information on resources available. A few interviewees said, though, that all they desired from the government was to be left alone. A Guatemalan banker quoted his father as saying, in a period of dictatorship, "We want to be forgotten." A favorable "climate" for private enterprise was frequently desired: "no giving away or taking away" (commercial manager, Mexico) and no restrictive labor legislation. A Guatemalan merchant said:

The state should leave private enterprise alone and only control social and working conditions. The state interferes with everything here without having, at least, experts to do it. There are impracticable laws which are never repealed, for example, on profit limitations.

Credit facilities at reasonable rates, especially for long-range purposes, were almost generally considered a task for government agencies in the absence of adequate credit supply from private sources. The Banco do Nordeste do Brasil was almost universally approved of in that region. Nearly all of the outspoken critics of state intervention among Venezuelan managers were found to use extensively investment funds supplied by *Fomento* and to find this use entirely compatible with abstract criticism of state intervention. However, political yardsticks and favoritism in public credits to private enterprise, sometimes referred to as *compadrazgo político*, were criticized everywhere.

Tariff protection likewise was almost universally approved and it was often claimed that without it no industry could develop or survive in the country concerned. Even among the unprotected industries there seemed to be no general resistance to tariff policy and no free-trade mentality corresponding to any laissez-faire attitude on the domestic level. But an industrial manager in Guatemala

said, "I think tariffs are of no use here as long as consumers
have no money. Low prices are much more important. For
these views some people call me a Communist!"

A public enterprise manager in Mexico commented on
the relationship between state and private enterprise as
follows:

Private enterprise is often overemphasized. *We* started the development of [a specific product], even produced the equipment. We then offered it to private enterprise but haven't found
much response. Private enterprise often has a very difficult role
in facing market and investment problems. Long-range thinking is a more logical task for the government. The state should
be the catalyst for economic development. A good dose of
estatismo cannot be avoided in a dynamic process. The state
should *start* enterprises, then turn them over to private interests.
It should be the nucleus of development. Some private companies fight us and bankers think our projects cost too much
and will fail, but many like to sell to us.

It is interesting to compare this with a statement from a
former president of the Cámara Nacional de la Industria de
Transformación, a Mexican employers' association:

There is no doubt that in our country the initiative for industrialization came from the government leaders; it did not result
from private initiative. It is likewise unquestionable that the
idea spread rapidly and that businessmen are rapidly falling in
line, in those groups which go along with the desire for industrialization.[10]

4. *Development incentives* beyond credit facilities and
tariffs were also considered by most a necessary function of
the state, though there were some warnings against breed-

[10] José Domingo Lavín, *En la Brecha Mexicana* (México, D. F.:
Edición y Distribución Ibero Americana de Publicaciones, 1948),
pp. 97ff.

ing "artificial" industries. It was usually taken for granted that new enterprises should remain tax-free for a substantial period but there was also a good deal of feeling that there should be no direct taxation of either new or old businesses. The justification, or rationalization, at the root of such tax ideas was the necessity of capital formation in the interest of greater private investment. However, specific ideas on how to channel untaxed profits definitely into new investment were rare. The Alliance for Progress idea of taxing those who could afford to pay was not particularly popular in general as is shown in the next chapter, and was definitely rejected with regard to industrial or commercial profits. On the other hand, there was a good deal of preoccupation with government deficits. But the latter were thought of mostly in terms of spending or administrative inefficiency, not in terms of inadequate tax revenues.

5. *Development planning* on the part of governmental agencies was considered legitimate and essential in some, but not all, areas to the extent that it was known. Such words as *coordinador, regulador, fomentador,* and *estimulador* were frequently used to classify the role of the state. The prevailing idea was that the government should provide the framework, infrastructure, supervision, and guidance which would result in the integrated growth of agriculture and industry, but that the main part of economic development remained a task for private enterprise. Planning in the sense of stimulation for definite activities or regions was thus distinguished from interference, *planeamiento* from *planismo*.

The role of the state must be seen in a very flexible way, without any orthodoxy. There cannot be any free enterprise without state planning at the same time. I am opposed to hostile business attitudes toward the state. But there should be no state intervention of the kind which displaces private initiative. (Mining executive, Mexico.)

There is no continuity in government policy on economic development here. They only speak of it in an abstract way, don't know what to emphasize and what to do. (Industrial manager, El Salvador.)

In Venezuela, many managers emphasized the necessity for the Government to *define* the intended future roles of private and public action, respectively. One private industrial manager went considerably beyond this but represents an exception:

Businessmen must get away from the negation of the state's existence and from considering it like a foreign intruder. The state has a positive function in establishing equality of opportunity, also in providing extensive capital where it does not exist privately. The thought that the state can do nothing better than to turn over its enterprises to private ownership is absurd. Planning is indispensable.

In Northeastern Brazil, SUDENE (Superintendency for the Development of the Northeast) was criticized by a number of interviewees on political or ideological grounds but was approved of by most as a planning agency. The most frequent criticism expressed was that there was too little actual execution of its plans and not enough interest in the human aspects of development such as rural cooperatives. Regional planning on the part of the governmental agencies was also favored in various other areas. At times, however, this desire was presented in a sectionalist spirit: some Northeastern Brazilians resented São Paulo "imperialism" and certain business managers in Ceará had similar resentments toward Pernambuco even though both areas are ordinarily considered parts of the same region.

6. *Political yardsticks* were used by many interviewees in answering the question about the economic role of the state. It was said many times that by far the greatest contribution to economic development which the government could make would be by running its own affairs—with finance and justice given as frequent examples—in an efficient, democratic, and honest manner; otherwise valid government tasks will be carried out badly or not at all. The belief that government politicians and economists basically do not understand business management was fairly widespread, and *restrictive* price controls were quite unpopular. Impediments to industrial, commercial, and agricultural improvements and innovations from the time-honored dependence on political favors were often cited. So was the need for the creation of "confidence," political stability, and a civil service with objective standards of conduct.

Such political reforms, we repeat, were suggested as the most essential precondition of *economic* development. A Mexican *abogado* with widespread business interests said that he was a friend of many high government servants including presidents, but an enemy of "government" in the sense of a general principle. The judgment of each person on the economic role of the government was colored by his political and ideological preconceptions in general.

The problem is the egoism of the public administrator, his will to achieve power by using other people's money. I was Minister for a few weeks, but could not take the way in which they work in public offices. My family thought I was *loco* anyway to enter into politics; it was against the entire family tradition. But things have begun to improve in the Government, there are *some* good people there and it should be possible at some future date for efficient executives to participate in it. (Industrial manager, Venezuela.)

Government and Development

7. *Land reform*, or some kind of basic social change centered on agrarian conditions, was mentioned in various areas as the most important contribution the state could make to economic development, but specific ideas about it varied greatly in detail and were completely absent in some places. As indicated earlier, Mexican business managers commented with great frequency on a need for basic changes in the *ejido* system including its political misuses and educational shortcomings, and not a few suggested to scrap this system in favor of individual peasant landownership. In Chile, where very few interviewees in 1959–1960 had even mentioned the agrarian problem, the atmosphere had changed considerably by the time of the 1963 reinterviews. In Guatemala it was repeatedly claimed that utilization of unused land was more important than ownership changes. In El Salvador, Argentina, and Uruguay there was relatively little mention of land reform as a government function. In Northeast Brazil there was, but only in the sense of opening up new land and creating individual peasant holdings there, not in the sense of splitting up efficient large estates.

In those areas where this possible function of government was on the managers' mind they mostly thought of financial, legal, and technological changes in agriculture as a necessary procedure in order to include the *campesino* into the national consumers' market.

As long as the subhuman conditions among the rural population are not corrected, there can be no real industrial progress. People are dying of hunger. The agrarian policy must be corrected, guarantees of ownership are necessary. This will give the individual more dignity. The country is now in a "false" phase of industrialization. For whom are we producing? (Industrial manager, Mexico.)

111

8. *Private contribution to public development policy* was not a matter of wide concern. How did private enterprise itself propose to participate in a fruitful development policy of the government? The state was mostly thought of as someone to get things from, not someone to contribute to, and nationalism was interpreted by some in similar terms. Being aided or subsidized, for that matter, was seldom associated with bureaucratic government intervention, and the latter was criticized in an abstract way with only rare references to past business abuses or demands which might have encouraged it.

The most affirmative contribution to development policy that was encountered in the interviews was the interest of individual managers and some business organizations in better training opportunities for executives. (See Chapter III.) These facilities, it is true, were mainly thought of in terms of the interest of private firms themselves. But there was some realization that such an initiative might be in the public interest as well and that training facilities not necessarily needed to be supplied or financed by the state.

On the other hand, real negativism toward the state or uncompromising laissez-faire thinking seemed confined to a group of *neoliberales* in Venezuela and a rather limited representation in some other countries such as Mexico and Guatemala. In support of this view it was said that it applies *especially* to less developed countries because their new start gives them greater choice regarding the kind of economic principles they want to adopt, and because their chief problem is to create new wealth not just to redistribute the old one.

Even in Venezuela, however, the sizable antistate sector of the business community along with most other people tended to recognize a certain social obligation of private enterprise to reinvest its profits in line with the national development program. In the meantime, the spread of the *Dividendo Voluntario para la Comunidad* movement has confirmed this tendency.

Only a small group maintained that it is no one else's business what a firm does with its profits and that *en-richissez-vous* is the best development policy. Such rigid interpretation of the Mont Pèlerin movement—an international grouping of neoliberals in the laissez-faire sense—in which some of the interviewees were active is seldom implemented on the practical level. Analytic, detached thinking about the *reasons*, past or present, for the strong state intervention or for the wide public support it enjoys has remained rare. Likewise, few understand the reasons why people in their countries have tended to be disappointed both with private and public enterprise. Retreat into a wishful world of Free Enterprise occurs largely under the influence of the official line of North American business. Musings on social utility and responsibility of private enterprise in their own country relieve some others momentarily of an underlying lack of belief in what they are doing.

On the other hand, state intervention is often accepted after the event, at least, if it has had any beneficial effects for private enterprise. Most of the enterprise managers interviewed, at any rate, were actually more opposed to bad government practices than to government as an economic influence in general or as a development planner.

I do not believe in liberal capitalism as such. The Government should create the right atmosphere, along with social justice and social security. I definitely favor the latter. Impractical idealism can ruin the economy, though. (Industrial manager, Mexico.)

Although there has been much preoccupation with communism or *castrismo*, there has thus far been relatively little concern with the public image of private business, and less worry about lack of social approval than exists among enterprise managers of more developed countries.[11] The limited extent of real social malaise may have encouraged optimism and investment even in areas where complaints about political instability have been high. But this limitation probably has also contributed to the lag of concern about the best contribution of private enterprise to economic development. Those development needs that are seen in specific terms are usually related just as strongly to a positive developmental role of the government even when this role is in part associated with inflationary tendencies.

In summary, the development stage of the country concerned is usually seen in terms of an incipient development which leaves a great many things to be done. In the view of most managers this stage requires a positive development role of the state which is to complement private enterprise by providing good government, education, agrarian reform, industrial stimuli, and monetary stability. Moderate inflation is mostly considered an inevitable effect of economic development with some good and some bad aspects. State enterprises are often criticized but more so in a pragmatic than a dogmatic vein. Infrastructure and other aids to private enterprise, as well as development planning of a guiding and coordinating type are regarded as legiti-

[11] For a comparison with European experiences during the nineteenth century, Alexander Gerschenkron, "Social Attitudes, Entrepreneurship, and Economic Development," in *Economic Backwardness in Historical Perspective* (Cambridge, Mass.: Harvard University Press, 1962), Chap. 3.

mate, perhaps indispensable, activities of the state. Systematic thinking about the corresponding contribution of private enterprise to public development policy remains fairly rare.

VII

The Foreign Role in National Economic Development

IN the preceding chapters we have discussed the ways in which enterprise managers in Latin America perceive the domestic possibilities of private and public effort combined in each country, in relation to its development needs. How do these managers, in comparison, see the possible contribution of foreign participation in the economic development of their country through either investment funds or aid brought in from outside sources?

Foreign Investment

We shall first discuss the views encountered concerning the role of foreign investment, in response to the question "What do you think is the future of foreign investment in this country from its own point of view?" It was made clear to each interviewee that the question should *not* be answered from the point of view of prospective foreign investors.

The general attitude toward foreign investment appeared at first almost entirely favorable. With the exception of a few areas such as Bahia in Northeast Brazil which had had little firsthand experience in this field and of some individual managers elsewhere who held no independent opinions in this respect, practically everybody thought that his country needed capital from any source quite badly. It was also felt that foreign investment would remain a necessity for a long time from the country's own point of view, though domestic capital formation might be even more important.

When, however, a probing question was added concerning the preferable forms of foreign investment, an array of important, even crucial, qualifications was presented by many respondents. Those who would unconditionally welcome foreign capital were a minority in every country covered. The qualifications offered can be grouped as follows:

(a) *Know-how*. It was frequently pointed out that money import as such had very limited uses unless it was accompanied by the importation of industrial or other know-how of a kind that was not readily available in the country. Private technical assistance, therefore, was seen as the main value in foreign investment. Some managers thought that loans to domestic enterprise from foreign sources, accompanied by technical assistance, was all that was needed. Others, however, wanted foreign capital precisely to produce in the country, not merely to advise, finance, or assemble.

(b) *No special privileges.* This theme was stressed by very many managers in every country but most emphatically so in the more developed areas of Mexico, Colombia, Chile, Argentina, and Brazil. The general idea was that the foreign-owned enterprise in question should be prepared to take risks (even though, as was shown earlier, many of the managers interviewed were not very eager to apply this principle to their own firms) that it should not be put from the outset into a favored position by special treatment on the legal or administrative levels with respect to taxation, tariffs, or foreign-exchange transfers, and that it should be expected to comply fully with domestic legislation, the obvious assumption being that domestic enterprise did. Any political pull through influencing judges, congressmen, or ministers was also frequently classified as a thing of the past that should no longer be attempted.

Some interviewees admitted that in the absence of special privileges or at least guarantees, the attraction of their country to foreign investors might not be strong enough to cope with the capital needs. However, only a few seemed inclined to compromise basically for this reason. An industrial promoter in Mexico claimed that North American investors abroad are still *colonialistas* who want to dictate whereas he himself, in the investment he holds in the United States, is only interested in dividends and capital gains.

(c) *No unequal competition.* Not a few interviewees felt that foreign capital should be encouraged to enter only those fields of business where there was no established domestic production or commerce yet; in other words, that it should be *complementary* to domestic activities, not *absorbente.* One reason given was that there were so many new opportunities waiting and that, at the same time, the total existing market was so small that there was no valid reason for foreigners to compete with established domestic enterprises. Another reason cited was that North American or British firms with the backbone of a safely established mass market at home or in other parts of the world could afford to undersell domestic firms almost indefinitely and that the latter could not develop or survive in the face of such competition on unequal terms. A small minority however, felt that competition from any source was needed and helpful in stimulating efficiency.

(d) *No political domination.* A distinct group of interviewees in various countries saw the main hazard of foreign investment not in economic but in political factors. It was pointed out repeatedly that the past aspirations and practices of foreign companies in dominating the politics and, indeed, the whole life pattern of people in the Caribbean "banana republics," for instance, had long since become unacceptable. Foreign investors should come into a country these days only if they realize that governments, political parties, dictators, and military *juntas* can no longer be bought freely and that such attempts merely arouse left-wing nationalism. A public-enterprise manager in Mexico felt that the country could *afford* more foreign investment now—without privileges and with mixed management, though—since it had sufficiently grown in strength and independence to frustrate any attempt at political interference.

(e) *No exploitation.* In a somewhat similar vein but with greater economic emphasis it was said repeatedly that foreign investment was welcome as long as it was not exploitative or colonialist.

When foreign investment takes the economic surplus away it is harmful; when it does not it is beneficial. It is the reinvestment of profits which decides this issue. (Banker and promoter, Mexico.)

Exploitation was rarely associated with low wages, poor working conditions, or unfavorable union relations and employment policies. Traditionally, few Latin American businessmen have worried much about such matters themselves and only recently have there been some signs of change. In most cases the term exploitation referred to draining off the resources of a country without offering it corresponding benefits.

This included, especially, the concentration of foreign investment on extractive industries—taking irreplaceable oil or copper out of the soil and out of the country, and reinvesting the profits abroad. Other statements referred to misdirection of national development in the interest of foreign investors, for example, by having railroads built merely from harbors to foreign-owned mines instead of developing an integrated network. The economic merits of such arguments will not be discussed here but it is important to note that in the light of this investigation the perception of foreign investment as potentially exploitative is by no means confined to left-wing labor leaders or revolutionaries.[1]

[1] Compare ¿ *Qué Opina la Iniciativa Privada Acerca de las Inversiones Extranjeras?*, Confederación de Cámaras Industriales de los Estados Unidos Mexicanos (1957). For this and the following three sections, see Claude McMillan, Jr., Richard F. Gonzales with Leo G. Erickson, *International Enterprise in a Developing Economy: A Study of U.S. Business in Brazil* (East Lansing, Mich.: Bureau of Business and Economic Research, Michigan State University, 1964); Wolfgang Friedmann and George Kalmanoff, *Joint International Business Ventures* (New York: Columbia University Press, 1961). Also Joseph Grunwald, "Why Not Invest in Latin America?" *Harvard Business Review*, Vol. 41, No. 6 (Nov.–Dec., 1963), pp. 123–128.

(f) *Sound financial practices.* A variety of financial conditions were cited as essential in order to make foreign investment beneficial to the recipient nation. Some interviewees found the use of scarce local credit and capital resources by foreign companies especially objectionable since foreign business activities in a less developed country should tend to increase not to reduce the credit and capital supply. Others had serious reservations about investment of the hit-and-run or speculative types which would come for a year or two, perhaps in the form of stock transactions, and then pull out suddenly thus adding to the foreign-exchange problem. The suggestion was made that nationals should have the option to acquire foreign assets when the latter are not properly used. (Industrialist, El Salvador.)

A more emphatic and widespread requirement cited concerned the reinvestment in the country of profits made there. It was made rather clear that many enterprise managers no less than other groups now are opposed to any extensive exportation of profits by foreign-owned firms. The latter are increasingly expected to keep reinvesting their profits as a general principle and to integrate their new investments into the national development program. Here again requirements toward foreign investors often seemed to be stricter than those which enterprise managers were ready to impose on their own companies.

(g) *Roots within the country.* Pursuing a similar trend of thought, some interviewees defined the most desirable kind of foreign investor as the one who comes to the country with his capital and know-how in order to stay there for good. His "foreign" investment thus is gradually converted into "national." As mentioned earlier, a few respondents represented the other extreme; namely, preference for foreign loans to domestic firms without any operational ambition on the part of the foreign capitalist. It was occasionally mentioned, however, that if foreign funds of the former kind, investment with increasing roots in the country, was not available, loans might be the next best alternative in preference to business operations managed essentially from the outside. Wholly owned branches of foreign companies were usually regarded as a business form of the past, though one manager of such a firm in Mexico proudly pointed out that its entire personnel, including himself, was Mexican. The foreign-born head of a largely foreign-owned company in Mexico considered some degree of nationalism a necessary and healthy safeguard against foreign capital domination.

(h) *Joint business ventures.* Some countries have legislation which requires a sizable proportion or majority of the shares to be owned by nationals, but such provisions are often circumvented. At any rate, there was almost complete consensus regarding the superiority of mixed foreign-domestic enterprise over the purely foreign type. It was pointed out that foreign capital meets with a far better political and emotional reception when joining forces with domestic, and that the combination of foreign capital and technical experience with local knowledge of markets and customs produces a very promising business operation. Some respondents added, however, that the local participants should always own the majority interest or that, at least, they should be "respected." Examples of foreign private cooperation with public enterprises in Latin America were cited as another possibility for future expansion.

When the question was raised whether such joint ventures should also include a joint structure of management, only the interviewees from firms which already had such a structure gave a clearly affirmative answer, mostly by pointing to the favorable experience of their own firm.

Foreign Role in Economic Development

Apart from dividends we are very public-relations minded. I myself keep in the background, though. Our public relations man is a Mexican with many contacts in the government and abroad. Mexicans are very sensitive, but we have been treated well. Investors should come in and start working, after first investigating the field. The outlook is no worse than it was, and better than under Cárdenas. Our experience with mixed capital *and* management has been good. Efficiency alone, regardless of nationality, decides our executive selection. The top man and the treasurer are usually European, though. The stockholders like it this way. (Manager, European-born, of a largely foreign-owned industrial company in Mexico.)

In many cases the response to the question about joint *management* was either negative or hesitant. *Some* representation of the foreign investors in the management was usually considered appropriate, even necessary. But it was clear that many of the native-born managers did not relish especially the thought of having to work together with, or possibly being displaced by, foreign executives with superior training if lesser knowledge of local conditions and mentality including "idiosyncrasies, the domestic way of life, market psychology, personnel administration, laws." (Industrialist, El Salvador.) Joint business ventures were thus thought of by many as a combination of capital and know-how but not of actual management. There was also some criticism of North American prejudice, especially in the smaller companies, against native executive personnel even when good persons were available. On the other hand, a Mexican university economist commented:

Under present conditions foreign investment happens anyway. Even if it is not the most desirable way to develop the country one must accept it. The foreign capital element always dominates, even when officially there is a combination of forces— partly because of the attitudes of the Mexican businessmen.

(i) *Effects of Latin American integration.* Only a few interviewees had given thought to the possible effects of a Latin American Common Market upon either foreign investment in their own countries or new investment opportunities for themselves in other parts of Latin America. An exception was provided by one major enterprise in Chile. In fact, not much thinking had been done on the Common Market in general as will be shown later. This lag was in contrast to the *Central American* integration which had clearly stimulated new thinking and, to some extent, activity among enterprise managers in El Salvador and Guatemala. Such contemplation as was encountered regarding future Common Market prospects was focused far more on its trade and migration effects than on new investment opportunities. Neither a great flow of North American or European capital to the entire area nor an interchange of investment funds among its own member countries appeared to have reached the stage of concrete thinking. This latter problem will presently be examined from an additional angle.

Likewise the Alliance for Progress, which is discussed in the next major section, had not been thought of as a great new source of investment flow from the outside, and probably quite rightly so. This appeared to be in contrast with some highly optimistic expectations in the United States concerning new investment opportunities that the Alliance would open up all over Latin America.

(j) *Nationalization, foreign capital, and development needs.* As mentioned earlier, those who commented on nationalization measures (even though no direct question to this effect was asked) were unanimously opposed to the confiscatory kind of nationalization. Mostly nationalization of foreign property with compensation was disapproved, too, insofar as the general principle was concerned, but some interviewees felt that *basic* resources such as oil and power should be owned nationally, either publicly or privately. Implicitly, at least, they seemed prepared to go along with nationalization in those fields.

Some of those who approved of foreign investment in general felt that its continuance and expansion in the country depended of necessity on its integration with national development planning so that any drain on scarce resources for nondevelopmental purposes would be avoided. Cola drinks were a popular example given for the kind of foreign investment that was considered useless from the viewpoint of a national development policy. The recipient country was to "select" the foreign investments it needed for specific development purposes.

This leaves the question whether the enterprise managers interviewed had thought of their own companies or business groupings as possible investors in other Latin American countries in line with *their* development programs. The answer is that such mention was rare, though one of the Argentinian companies included in the sample had a subsidiary in Chile, for instance. In general there was little evidence of any intended interchange of capital among Latin American countries on a substantial scale, again with the possible exception of the Central American area in a limited way. On the other hand, interviewees in every area visited mentioned investment (or "hot" money) held in the United States, Switzerland, or other developed countries by individuals and business groups from their own country which could ill afford such drain on the national development effort. This paradox was mostly explained by the prevailing uncertainty in the country's political, social, or economic conditions.

Enterprise in Latin America

Attitudes toward foreign capital thus were found to be mostly favorable in a general way, but legal and other qualifications were made by the great majority of the managers interviewed. Special privileges available to foreign interests and exploitation of basic resources by them were especially unpopular, and reinvestment in the country of profits made by foreign investors was strongly favored. Examples of inter-American investment were few and no movement in this direction on a substantial scale was discernible at the time of the interviews.

Foreign Development Aid

In comparison with the domestic effort and foreign investment, respectively, how did the Latin American enterprise managers view the role of foreign aid, especially the Alliance for Progress, in the economic development of their countries? Which forms of foreign development aid did they consider the most fruitful?

To begin with, when asked about foreign aid a sizable number of interviewees answered once more in terms of foreign *investment*. In other words, the concept of "aid" was not familiar or clear to everybody. Only when a probing question about the Alliance for Progress was added did the meaning of the question become clearer to these interviewees, at least to the extent that they were informed about the Alliance.

Among those who were reasonably familiar with the facts and problems of foreign development aid, nearly everybody considered such aid necessary or, at least, desirable for the foreseeable future. Some said that Latin America "deserves it" as a good customer and supplier of raw materials to the wealthier nations. There was much less agreement on the *kind* of aid that was most important.

Some interviewees thought of aid primarily in terms of "money" in general or, more specifically, foreign-exchange grants or long-term loans on favorable terms. But there was a significant group who felt that technical assistance to industry and agriculture was the most urgent and effective kind of aid. Still others placed the emphasis on aid for social improvements, especially education and health.

Although the question asked did not refer to any particular source, the answers were given almost unanimously in terms of United States aid. It is possible, of course, that this was partly due to the nationality of the interviewer. In a few cases an additional reference was made to United Nations Technical Assistance or one of the UN specialized agencies such as the International Bank for Reconstruction and Development. There was no spontaneous mention of aid from European or Soviet sources.

Of those who had definite ideas on foreign aid nearly all pointed out in one way or another that aid should be offered strictly for well-defined development purposes not as a stopgap or present just to tie over a bankrupt or inefficient government. In some cases it was added that for precisely this reason *misguided* foreign aid had been quite harmful and had discredited the whole foreign-aid idea among the people.

When the conversation turned more specifically toward the Alliance for Progress (this, of course, was confined to the 1962 and 1963 interviews) the responses were more specific but even more varied. The main points made can be grouped as follows:

(a) *What IS the Alliance?* Even among informed people puzzlement about the basic meaning, purposes, and methods of the Alliance was frequent. The president of a small industrial firm in Guatemala had never talked to his son, the *gerente,* about the Alliance. To his mind, the old aid program had simply been renamed. Some managers professed to be unable to comment because they did not really understand the whole thing or its intended procedure. We are not referring here to the sizable group who said that they had not kept up with the news in this field and were lacking in factual information about the Alliance.

A few of the former group added that as nearly as they could make out the Alliance represented primarily a matter of public relations or a political measure in the interest of the United States, rather than real aid for Latin American development. The comment that the Alliance was more in the economic interest of the United States than that of the Latin American participants was also made a number of times. Such comments were made in a resigned, rather than a hostile, mood.

We are not anti-American; we need cooperation, but we are critical of U.S. shortcomings in the same way as we are of our own. (Industrial and commercial manager, Northeast Brazil.)

There also was occasional criticism of the entire "aid" concept in the sense of demoralizing handouts including food, save in an emergency, instead of mutual cooperation and long-range loans designed to support the domestic development aims.

Aid should put the recipient to work, not be offered as a gift. The *facility* of the aid is an evil. People will always ask for much but won't appreciate it. Only mutual aid programs have succeeded thus far. The *how* of this aid is decisive. You cannot export U.S. institutions. (Industrial manager, Guatemala.)

There were also some charges of demagoguery that was thought to prevail on both sides.

(b) *Good idea but ineffective.* One of the most frequent reactions was that the Alliance represented a fine impulse in a general sense but had thus far remained ineffective on the practical level, or that any such effects were not yet discernible in the area concerned. The feeling of "It sounds all right but I want to be shown" was widespread among enterprise managers in all the countries covered. An industrial manager in Mexico felt that the use of foreign aid should be supervised in the country by a committee of businessmen and public officials; people often do not know where the aid comes from, and "It is a shame to see how much vanishes (*se filtra*)." He felt, moreover, that aid to education, in particular, should be based on "Mexican solutions."

Some interviewees said that the Alliance was effective as a social but not as an economic program. A few thought the Alliance was ineffective because it was not really focused on the *ambiente* or the basic development of the economy, but that it could generate a change in mutual mentality. It was also recommended to emphasize long-run "bankers' loans" as a business proposition, though on favorable terms.

(c) *Too little money.* Sometimes skeptical feelings were expressed more specifically in approximately the following financial terms: "The idea is good, but how much money will actually reach each of the nineteen countries involved out of the generously allotted yet rather limited total budget?" These reactions, of course, expressed in turn an interpretation of the Alliance in purely financial terms, essentially as a new name for unilateral flow of aid funds from the United States to Latin America.

A more sophisticated form of this reservation tried to show that the aid allotted did not even make up for sudden drops in world market prices for coffee, sugar, copper, or other crucial export commodities. The United States was usually held responsible for such price reductions, though price *rises* were seldom booked to its credit. There seemed to be a widespread assumption that the United States had a political, if not moral, obligation to buy up any commodity which the other countries of the continent produced, regardless of whether it needed it or not, and to do so at constantly favorable prices.

Some interviewees, it is true, pointed to industrialization as the only real way out of the dilemma through growing diversification of production and exports. One, in El Salvador, suggested that future gains from higher coffee prices could be channeled into industrial investment. Another one in the same country thought that a U.S.–backed investment-insurance corporation, which would result in a return of domestic flight capital, would make the whole Alliance program superfluous.

(d) *Bureaucratic structure.* Another comment made a number of times was that the Alliance idea was better than its procedures or personnel. Some retailers commented that the most beneficial effect of the Alliance for them was the increase in business from selling to North American aid personnel. It was claimed that aid applications from either public or private enterprises were processed at a slow pace, that good development projects were held up, or that the preparation of some AID personnel was not up to the requirements.

The experts who come should stay long enough to be effective. They should know the background of the country, not mix it up with the United States. (Landowner and industrialist, Guatemala.)

Criticism was voiced, for instance, for trying to impose a balanced diet in the United States sense on people who much prefer an abundant supply of *tortillas* and *frijoles*.

(e) *More private enterprise.* A theme frequently heard suggested that the Alliance would have better and wider effect if the aid were channeled mainly to private enterprise, rather than to the government of each country. The justifications given for this view varied. Some enterprise managers were so convinced of the evil nature of the existing kind of government in their country (for reasons of its corruption, power politics, oppression, or radicalism) that they considered *any* aid to such a government a damaging influence.

Bureaucracy here has been strengthened by the U.S. Government through giving loans to our government. This practice fosters socialism and Communism. I don't know the reasons for this practice. My company hasn't got a penny from the Alliance. (Industrialist, Mexico.)

However, an industrialist in El Salvador commented,

Government-to-government loans, on principle, can be good if they are given for good purposes. Government is not necessarily bad; if it is, it's our fault.

An industrial manager in Chile (reinterview, 1963) said,

The Alliance is very good but it has been from government to government, and the Latin American governments do not represent any large sector of the people. It should be directed more toward contacts between citizens' groups and such so that the average person here *and* in the U.S. will think of it as something which concerns *him*.

Others used economic arguments by saying that aid to private, especially medium or small, enterprise was the most effective method of development, or that the productive structure of the country needed strengthening before any great advances in public welfare were possible. Few appeared to have any concrete ideas on how the U.S. Government could best deal directly with thousands of individual firms in each of the nineteen countries without encroaching upon the sovereign rights of national governments. About the only suggestion made was that the Alliance should encourage government-guaranteed long-range loans from U.S. private banks to local banks, both private and public, which would then pass on the money to landowners and industrialists on a long-range, low-interest basis. (Partner, agricultural company, Guatemala.) The Export-Import Bank was also mentioned occasionally as an example of sound practice in the private distribution of foreign loan funds.

(f) *Emphasis on private contacts.* In a similar but more specific vein some thoughts were presented on how to reshape the Alliance idea altogether so that its essence would be no longer a special kind of economic relations between the governments but rather a closer contact between business firms and other private groups of the member countries. Just how this could best be done seemed to remain unclear in the minds of most proponents. A few of them seemed to think of an extensive organization for technical assistance to be given from company to company on top of the accustomed flow of investment capital. One example given by a commercial manager in Mexico concerned extended insurance of private loans.

A few, however, thought more broadly in terms of organized "people-to-people" contact and aid, which would include not only business firms but civic and voluntary groups on both sides in a much larger degree than had been experienced in the past. In each case the prevailing attitude was that with the existing kind of government in most countries concerned, there was little hope in aid to governments but that the Alliance idea was quite adaptable to closer relations among private groups.

(g) *No strings attached.* While there was much criticism of aid addressed to the existing governments, there was even more frequent opposition to making changes in political and social institutions a condition of aid. Such opposition was expressed in a number of different ways. In Guatemala and El Salvador, for example, many interviewees were against the reforms proposed altogether. It was claimed that large landholders (or the rich in general) were being taxed directly or indirectly already and that further taxation would destroy the sources of investment funds. Likewise, there was supposedly not enough moral and educational background in the country to have an honest income tax. Business taxes might be all right for advanced economies but not for countries in the process of costly new industrialization, and military expenditures should be cut before introducing new taxes. Land reform in the sense of better marketing and mechanization was going on anyway, and any splitting up of large estates into inefficient *minifundia* could only interfere with the productivity effort.

Others stressed that both land reform and tax reform would require decades to be carried through while the need for foreign aid was urgent and that the Alliance, after all, should be prepared to take *some* risk. The third major requirement, a national development plan, also encountered the argument that perfectionism might cause intolerable delays in development aid. Generally, however, development planning was not opposed though some interviewees thought that such plans are seldom carried out. Interestingly, a Mexican government economist felt that the Alliance represented a doctrinaire generalization of the *Mexican* revolutionary experience in agrarian change and socio-economic development policy.

Some interviewees, it is true, showed a distinctly affirmative, even emphatic attitude toward the reform requirements of the Alliance, but the attitude of the majority could be summed up with "Just give us the money and no nonsense." Lack of tact in past U.S. aid activities was cited as reason why the United States had not received the gratitude it deserved, but it was also said that favors given are always resented by the recipient sooner or later.

(h) *Concept of their own role.* It was a small group of interviewees that pointed out succinctly and critically the prevailing mode of thinking toward the Alliance, a mode which characterized the majority of enterprise managers and probably of the general population. People tended to think of the Alliance in terms of "they," not "we." Interpretation of the Alliance as a *common* effort in which the Latin American people themselves must have the major share by carrying out necessary social reforms, mobilizing substantial development funds, and organizing their economy and way of life in an appropriate manner, was rare at the time of the investigation. The Alliance was thought of by most interviewees not as a mutual effort but as something brought to the country from the outside mainly under U.S. responsibility, if not as a generous condescending concession of Latin America to North American fears and security needs.[2] The difference between the Alliance for Progress and the AID was not always understood.

The small group referred to at the beginning of the

[2] "The Alliance for Progress must be a cooperative effort. Without the enthusiastic devotion of Latin American talents, energies, and resources to its purposes, no lasting results can be achieved." Lincoln Gordon, *A New Deal for Latin America: The Alliance for*

preceding paragraph can be exemplified by the following statements:

The Alliance is a great plan but it has been greatly misunderstood by *everybody* including the North Americans as just pouring in more money. It should mean our helping *ourselves*, with some complementary aid. (Industrialist, Mexico.)

Aid will not save us, but collaboration in an auxiliary sense is fine. "Aid" does not really exist and the Alliance is quite mythological. It cannot be applied rapidly because it would upset the national economy. Everything needs time. Mexico has already got the elements of economic development, they merely need to be complemented thoughtfully in a long-range way. "Aid" applies only to those who haven't got anything. (Manager, construction firm, Mexico.)

In other words, of those enterprise managers who had a clear concept of foreign aid and definitely related it to development, most thought that it represented a continuing need even though aid could easily be misused. The Alliance for Progress was not clear in its meaning to everybody and was sometimes seen in terms of U.S. interests chiefly. The general idea of the Alliance was widely approved, but many felt that there had been little practical effect yet as a result of inadequate funds, procedure, or personnel, and insufficient emphasis on private enterprise. Reform requirements as preconditions of aid were widely criticized. There was little concept of Latin American action as the mainstay of the Alliance, a concept which was subsequently going to be stressed at the November, 1963, meeting in São Paulo of the Inter-American Economic and Social Council.

Progress (Cambridge, Mass.: Harvard University Press, 1963), p. 10. Also Edward S. Mason, *Foreign Aid and Foreign Policy* (New York: Harper and Row, 1964), Chap. 4.

Enterprise in Latin America

Long-range Outlook and Latin American Integration

In comparison with the outlook for early development aid from the Alliance for Progress, how did enterprise managers evaluate, with a longer perspective, the prospects of Latin American economic integration?

In order to bring out the extent of long-range thinking in general, toward the end of the interview the question was asked, "What do you think will the economy of this country be like in twenty-five years or so?" The clearest result that emerged was the widespread lack of long-range thinking among the enterprise managers interviewed. The majority responded as if they had never thought in these terms before. They were surprised, sometimes bewildered, but usually stimulated by this question. Some refused to speculate because they felt the problem was beyond them. Others commented that they had their hands full just trying to survive and had not been able to think about a distant future. Still others said that they had no crystal ball, that the remote future depended on too many unknown factors, such as U.S and European politics, to be evaluated or that changes in today's world were so rapid that the future was inscrutable.

A substantial number, however, responded positively either because they had done long-range thinking before or because they felt sufficiently stimulated by the question. Long-range optimism was predominant among them even though some had commented adversely on the current situation or the problems facing the country. The reason given was either that one *had* to be optimistic these days in order to keep going or, more frequently, that the country concerned (and this was said in every country) had enormous resources—human, natural, or both. It was bound sooner or later, therefore, to start making fuller use of them, especially through industrialization and transition to the export of manufactured goods thus raising enormously its standard of living. A Mexican industrialist more cautiously expected his country to approach in twenty-five years the industrial and economic level of the poorer European nations. The most frequent profession of faith referred to the people and their basic intelligence and resourcefulness, and to the growing integration of the nation in question. The rise of a strong middle class was mentioned by some as a favorable trend both economically and politically.

Such optimism was often qualified by some "if" or other, understandably so in face of a long-range question. References to world conditions, especially the possibility of a nuclear war, were frequent and the optimistic type of predictions nearly always assumed that such a disaster could be averted. There were also some fears that certain sectors of the population, such as the Indians, might be left even farther behind than they are now, or that widespread praise of "the land of the future" in general might be an excuse for doing nothing.

A frequent reservation made referred to political developments in the nation itself. The economic outlook was deemed by most to be very favorable in the long run if only an honest and efficient government could be achieved, if excessive state intervention could be avoided, if the constant threat of military coups came to an end, and if political stability could finally be established.

Other qualifications made referred to the necessity of a well-thought-out development program that would stimulate the people to a real effort in the interest of systematic economic advancement over many years. Another precondition cited was greater consciousness on the part of private enterprise of the needs of the people. A Mexican mining executive said:

In Mexico, socialism could only come from Laredo [meaning from the United States]. The chief influence here will come from world trends. Perhaps there will be more state intervention, but I am not very worried about it if individual liberties are preserved. I am for better integration of the social forces. There will be an ever more planned economy but with growing participation of business. Business must assume social responsibility and justice.

The theme of promising economic growth being conditioned upon greater social responsibility of private enterprise was stressed on a few occasions. This, however, cannot yet be considered a general trend among Latin American enterprise managers.

Finally, some interviewees qualified their long-range optimism by saying that it assumed substantial and continuing development aid from outside. But the majority responded to the question in terms of the intrinsic resources of their country which were likely to be mobilized through domestic effort over the next two or three decades

As for Latin American economic integration, in most areas the outstanding result of adding this kind of question ("What about a Latin American Common Market?") to the one on long-range trends in general was to find a very limited amount of information at the disposal even of many well-educated and generally well-informed managers. Only a minority which had more or less direct contact with this problem individually or through their firms and trade groups had substantial knowledge of the steps already taken in this direction, especially LAFTA (Latin American Free Trade Area).

Things were found to be different, however, in Guatemala and El Salvador, where managerial reactions to the *Central American* Common Market including the Central American Bank for Economic Integration were definite and favorable, and where many managers and firms were making real adjustments to the new situation. "The size of the market and the competition are increasing. The great problem remains consumption." (Industrial manager, Guatemala.) These responses, it is true, were received before the military coups in Guatemala and Honduras.

Aside from this regional trend, there was little evidence that preparation for Latin American economic integration had substantially affected managerial decision-making, especially investment intentions. Certain firms in Chile and Argentina had become aware of mutual market possibilities and some managers interviewed quoted specific instances of an expanding geographic horizon for their business. Hesitant preparations for an inter-American reinsurance company were mentioned as an example. But in large areas managers had not taken future Common Market possibilities into account when making expansion decisions.

Hopes of a coming business expansion in the course of Common Market developments appeared to run highest in Mexico, where many industrialists felt to be in a sufficiently strong position to profit eventually from industrial integration and the new market opportunities involved. A Mexican industrialist described the reaction to such plans as initial indifference followed by skepticism followed by optimism. Another one anticipated much false, expensive industrialization everywhere out of nationalism, and "planning" *against* economic integration. But in Central America, as mentioned earlier, the regional arrangement made appeared to have had a real impact on the thinking of many businessmen who had long been resigned to a tiny domestic

market and had now begun to think in terms of a market of
12 or 13 million people. A merchant and industrialist in El
Salvador classified this development as "an industrial and
psychological explosion."

In 1960, fears of the "colossus of the North"—Brazil—
were running high in Chile, Argentina, and Uruguay. At
the time of the Chilean reinterviews in 1963, however,
expectations in that country appeared to be considerably
more favorable. The greatest hesitancy toward a Common
Market was encountered in Venezuela, where most interviewees with opinions said that the country could not very
well avoid joining it sooner or later, but that the transition
would be difficult because of the high level of wages and
prices in Venezuela. This fact was thought, for example, to
make it impossible for its textile industry to compete with
the Colombian in the absence of tariff protection.

It was repeatedly pointed out that a Latin American
Common Market presented problems entirely different
from those of the European Economic Community, about
which some interviewees professed to know more than
about the former. Compared with the diversified industrial
products of Western European countries, the Latin American nations were deemed to produce at this point too many
of the same goods, largely raw materials and foodstuffs, to
have much to offer to one another. Brazilians emphasized
the size of their own potential market which seemed to
make it pointless to look for opportunities in other countries in a similar stage of development. Various interviewees
stressed the fact that the nations concerned had had
entirely different monetary experiences so that integration
would require an intricate payment scheme, or that communications among them were too poor for real economic
integration. But some added that the progressing industrial-

ization of these nations might change this situation before long, and that integration of specific industries might be the most promising method for some time to come.

A few put their finger on what may well be the crux of Latin American economic integration: whether and how the industrial and other development plans of the participating countries could be coordinated in such a way that new industries, at least, would complement, rather than duplicate, each other. Steel and automobiles were mentioned as examples.

The Common Market could help in solving the population problem of Latin America through interchange of people and goods, and coordination of production. (Industrial manager, Mexico.)

An industrial manager in Chile (reinterview, 1963) suggested that the United States should get more involved in Latin American integration through corresponding allocation and coordination of investments in Latin America thus following through its cooperation ideas from Punta del Este, otherwise there would not be a Common Market.

In summary, the prevailing perception among Latin American managers of the foreign role in national economic development—foreign investment, aid, and economic integration combined—was found to be moderately optimistic, with a great many "ifs" and serious limitations of the economic information available to them. Certainly a definite contribution from foreign sources to the economic development of the nation, along with a combination of private and public initiative at home, was expected by a large segment of the managerial group.

Long-range thinking was not very frequent but such as there was tended to be optimistic, usually with qualifications concerning avoidance of war, political stability, a good development program, or outside aid. The outlook for Latin American economic integration likewise had entered into the thinking of a limited group only. It had had little effect on managerial decisions including those on future expansion, with the exception of Central America, where a more limited regional arrangement had achieved a noticeable effect on managerial thinking. Future steps toward Latin American economic integration will depend on overcoming the legacy of individualistic mistrust toward others and emphasizing inter-American investment along with a coordination of national development progress.

VIII

Implications for the Latin American Development Process

WHAT do the findings of this study suggest with regard to determining factors in the development process and to corresponding policies for socioeconomic development under Latin American conditions? Such implications of our investigation will be discussed in this summarizing chapter. Some of them were rooted in direct suggestions received from the more forward-looking enterprise managers interviewed. Others suggested themselves to the writer more indirectly as a result of the attitudes encountered in the managerial group in comparison with points of view of people from other socioeconomic groups.

Clearly enterprise management represents only one of several factors and groups that influence the development process. Peasant farming and rural traditions, labor unions and social movements, political and military power relations, and the international situation of the country and government concerned all are very important influences, too. But the attitudes and behavior of the incipient managerial groups *are* of great significance in national development planning in general, in the organization and financing of industrialization, in the incorporation of the major population groups into the national market, and in finding suitable forms of foreign participation in national development processes.

Enterprises are managed by people from a specific culture and social setting. An individual does not scrap his general framework of attitudes, motives, and emotions the moment he is appointed a manager. By the same token, the cultural setting and group belonging of an enterprise manager are likely to influence the specific pattern of his thinking and decision-making in the course of the economic development process. In other words, we have not been concerned in this study with an ideal manager assumed to behave in line with the requirements of an abstract "rational" logic or in accordance with rules elaborated by economists from the United States and Great Britain, for example, on the basis of their own education and life experience. We have been speaking here of actual human beings in specific Latin American countries, who serve in managerial functions—with all their strengths, weaknesses, skills, and limitations.

If it could be assumed that managers, given certain kinds of training, skills, or education in general, behaved in the same way no matter where these qualities were to be applied, every principle of management from the most advanced economies would automatically be applicable to the development process of less developed areas. The problem of the latter would merely be to have sufficient numbers of people trained in the managerial skills that have been developed in the West. No such assumption has been made here. We simply are concerned with the *extent* to which managerial skills or attitudes from advanced economies have proved applicable to Latin America in the course of its development process.

Cultural Variations in Managerial Attitudes toward Development

In their attitudes toward short-range profit maximization, toward the economic and noneconomic uncertainties and risks facing them, toward the government, and toward the prospects for economic development, the managers of each area investigated turned out to be definitely—though often unconsciously—influenced by the cultural setting and the prevailing system of values there.

In certain countries managers are more likely than in others to view the problems of their enterprises or the tasks of development policy as strictly national in character. In other words, the degree in which they see capital shortage or social radicalism, for instance, as "Chilean" rather than as "Latin American" or "developmental" varies considerably. So does their perception—optimistic, pessimistic, or detached—of national, cultural, or regional characteristics of the population that may influence the conduct of management and business. As was pointed out in Chapter II, the prevailing interpretation of such characteristics sometimes emphasizes dynamic, cooperative, and intelligent traits of the population; in other cases it concentrates on supposedly individualistic, careless, or apathetic attitudes of the people. A manager in São Paulo claimed, for instance, that the Brazilian reacts to sudden challenge like a race horse: he *dashes* to the goal, then collapses and may need months to recover; the tradition of steady work is still missing. Such perceptions and the cultural mentality which they express, are bound to color the managers' general view of the possibilities of economic development in the country concerned and of their own role in such development.

Cultural variations in the value system and interpretation of life within Latin America, as well as between the latter and other parts of the world, thus need to be taken into due account by public development policy in each country, especially in the timing of "sound" measures or the degree of pressure used in order to produce certain managerial responses. Public development planning must not assume that what is needed is chiefly a new set of laws or regulations modeled uniformly after experiences with management in more advanced countries. Even tax incentives and subsidies may merely be interpreted as handouts unless prevailing values favor the rise of systematic management or adjust themselves sufficiently to favor it.

External aid, similarly, may miss the point by merely sending foreign textbooks or management experts whose experience was acquired in Germany or the United States. There certainly is some area of general effectiveness for purely technical advice on production statistics or the use of business machines, for instance. But even here the possibilities are rather limited in the absence of a basic attitude that recognizes the importance of such values as "exactness" and "reliability."

Both public policy and foreign aid for economic development, therefore, should start out from the prevailing values in each country and utilize them as much as possible while encouraging a gradual change in those attitudes that are incompatible with economic development. Abstract organization charts are of little effect where management is based primarily on family relations and personal contacts. But these relations and contacts can be brought into a certain order and can be made subservient in some degree to the requirements of efficient management. In other words, to examine in each case the probable effect of development measures, especially those directed at efficient management, upon the established values and ways of thinking looks like a far more promising procedure than to apply blindly to each Latin American country the technical principles of management derived from different cultural spheres.

Restating the point, there are some cultural variations affecting management among the Latin American countries and many more between Latin America as a whole and other parts of the world. A number of specific differences that are perceived by Latin American enterprise managers, or appear to affect them were discussed in Chapter II. A more detailed examination of cultural variations within Latin America must be left to the anthropologists.

Certainly all this should not lead to the extreme assumption that there are *only* variations among the values and attitudes of population groups in general and enterprise managers in particular. In fact, the question will perhaps be raised at this point whether development policy really needs to consider sociocultural variables in the attitudes and initial behavior of managers in a newly developing country.

The answer would be negative if we could simply assume that these countries are today passing through stages of management that closely parallel the earlier economic history of the now developed nations. This is not

the place for a systematic comparison of historical development patterns. It would be difficult, however, to prove
more than a superficial similarity between contemporary
Latin American attitudes toward executive selection and
training, competition, productivity, or the other factors
discussed in the preceding chapters and business attitudes in
Western European countries when *they* were underdeveloped, say, at the beginning of either the Commercial or the
Industrial Revolution. The answer to the question just
mentioned will, therefore, be affirmative if our evidence
indicates that newly developing nations today experience
largely different trends due to the time elapsed and an
accelerating demonstration effect, and that some influence
of their earlier cultural heritage persists even in the face of
industrialization.

It will be shown in the following section that actual indications of attitudinal change among Latin American managers and of an abandonment of their earlier preconceptions have thus far been confined largely to technical or
peripheral aspects of their behavior.

The Nature of Management in Latin America

In the light of the investigation described in the preceding chapters and the cultural variations just mentioned,
what generalizations can be made concerning the present
meaning and role of enterprise management in Latin America? How much active participation in the development
process of his country can be expected from the manager in
that part of the world? What can the study of Latin
American management contribute to our understanding of
development processes there in a more general way?

The people who run enterprises in Latin America today
offer an amazing variety of practices and viewpoints. This

is true not only according to the nation and area but according to the size and age of the enterprise and the non-economic (as well as economic) status striving of the managers. The fact that the managerial groups in many countries of Latin America contain a stronger foreign-born and urban element than the general population fosters in them frequent feelings of alienation and insecurity which invite status assertion.

The public role of management organizations also varies widely. A few are quite influential, but there is hardly a country in Latin America where any one trade association or group can rightly claim to speak for management as a whole or to represent it in discussions on economic development. The atomization of managerial groups and firms, which can be explained from the feudal legacy, brief industrial experience, and individualism of enterprise managers, remains quite widespread.

The very meaning of "management" in Latin America has often been subject to ethnocentric misunderstandings elsewhere. Management in that part of the world rarely represents scientific, clocklike, rational decision-making even in its intention, let alone its practice. Conceptual confusion is widespread between *empresa* and *empresario*, between ownership and management, and between private (or "free") enterprise and the professional managerial function that exists under almost any kind of ownership arrangement today.

In extreme cases such as the sugar interests in Northeast Brazil, a whole generation of owners was raised in the belief that they as the masters did not need to know "management," and that they had a natural right to get guaranteed high prices without worrying about productivity or understanding it. This generation now discovers with surprise that some people would like to see changes in the established land conditions, but it does not really understand what these people want. The younger generation, too, was raised in the *usina* atmosphere, though many of them were subsequently sent by their families to Europe in order to study the humanities or to play. Interviews with representatives of this business group brought very little evidence of attitudinal change.

There is no lack of criticism of such attitudes on the part of other business groups in various countries, and there is a thin layer of U.S.-trained, mostly younger managers who would like more or less to imitate North American ways or ideologies, but such resemblance has in many cases remained superficial. Intellectual and emotional isolation of enterprise managers from the government, the university students, and the workers is frequent.

As was pointed out in the first chapter, the Latin American manager is still mostly owner, co-owner, or representative of family interests in the enterprise or in a whole group of enterprises which often are not functionally related. The selection and promotion of executives is rarely guided by purely objective criteria, more often by family contacts and influences as was shown in Chapter III. It is only very recently that such background or purely practical experience within the enterprise concerned have begun to be considered insufficient and to be bolstered by more systematic executive training in the country or abroad.

Within the traditional and still prevailing socioeconomic pattern, the factory, store, *hacienda*, bank, political party, ministry may thus be merely different angles from which to look at a family-rooted power structure which is at once agrarian, financial, industrial, social, political, perhaps even diplomatic or religious. Such a conglomerate is not to be confounded with the logic of upstream or downstream integration, though the former *sometimes* occurs when a merchant starts producing some of the goods he has been selling.

Under these conditions, decision-making in the enterprise is even more frequently influenced by nonfinancial considerations there than it is in more developed countries, though such influences are not always conscious. The urge for high family status may be at the root of a decision to add a bank, for example, to older land holdings and industrial interests of the family even though the financial case for a new bank may be doubtful. A *nouveau riche* family with commercial enterprises may try to add to its prestige in the traditional manner (or else evade taxes) by acquiring an *hacienda* even though the latter offers no promising profit outlook. The class roots of the managerial group and the barriers facing many a potential entrepreneur for this reason explain in part the widespread quest for government positions among the new middle classes.

Long-range thinking with the corresponding kind of decisions is still fairly rare among Latin American managers as was shown in Chapter VII. Managerial decisions, therefore, are mostly directed at almost immediate results allowing only for the inevitable construction period of a new plant. Although complaints about the irremediable smallness of the market in a poor country persist, consumers somehow are also assumed to be anxiously waiting for any product that is newly offered. Expansion decisions, therefore, can supposedly be riskless. Conscious import substitution is unfamiliar to many as a general concept, but if a foreign product has aroused the buying intentions already and the market is there, why postpone profit or enter upon risky ventures in other fields of business? And how could any such course be justified in terms of the family's security and status in the community, unless such needs are from the outset at the root of hazardous decisions of the type described above—or else, unless unmitigated speculation in the sense of time-honored gambling habits is involved, in contradiction to the avoidance of calculated risk on the business level?

Managerial thinking and behavior thus is quite often unrelated to national development needs or programs. It might again be argued that this way of thinking simply represents an early stage of enterprise management, rather than a Latin American peculiarity, and that it took North American and Western European managers quite a long time, too, to build up even a moderate degree of development-mindedness. Although there is a certain element of truth in such explanations, any assumption that management in Latin America will of necessity follow in full, sooner or later, either the abstract or the practical patterns of Western Europe or North America would be rather shaky. It is true that to *some* extent, especially in the purely technical aspects of management such as budgeting, cost accounting, and inventory control, this is taking place already but much of this imitation has thus far remained on the surface.

At this point the diversified but mostly not logically structured enterprise of family-related nature still prevails in Latin America even though its legal form increasingly tends to be the *sociedad anónima* as was pointed out in Chapter I. Genuine corporate equity ownership with wide distribution of shares and a constant, functioning public market for them remains the exception. This investigation offers no conclusive evidence that this represents merely an historical lag behind North American or Western European patterns.

Emphasis on the strength of cultural values and traditions, and discussions of the persistency of certain attitudes which impede a "modernization" of managerial behavior in Latin America according to Western standards, always are in danger of being interpreted as an invitation to conservatism or inertia. If the cultural heritage tends to obstruct any real attitudinal change among enterprise managers, why not just accept their traditional "inefficiency" as a limiting factor of economic development?

This, of course, is not at all the meaning of the data obtained in this investigation, of their interpretation in the preceding chapters, or of the policy suggestions that are to follow in Chapter IX. We may amplify our meaning as follows.

The institutional and attitudinal framework which was encountered among Latin American enterprise managers in the course of this study, especially with reference to development needs, is not yet very conducive to rapid economic development. At the same time it is characterized by considerable rigidity and persistence. Adaptation to North American and Western European principles of managerial behavior, beyond the level of courtesy, superficial imitation, or techniques has been confined to a small number of corporations, though window-dressing among the others has been fairly frequent.

All this does not suggest that attitudinal change among Latin American managers is impossible. It does indicate that such attitudinal change will be gradual and that its effectiveness will depend on understanding modification of managerial principles and techniques from more advanced economies in each country and culture. In other words, the *how* will often be more important than the *what* in implementing the policies suggested. Attitudinal change is no more impossible in Latin America than anywhere else, but it is always slow and can never be confined to mere emulation of other cultures or economic systems. There are, it is true, some impressive signs of attitudinal differences between the old and the new generations of managers.

What will be the outcome of such changes when they occur? Some of the Latin American management attitudes encountered in this study should, and in all probability will be modified gradually as a result both of structural changes such as industrialization and land reform, and of conscious public policies. Latin American management will then become somewhat more similar to management in the United States or Great Britain than it is now, but it cannot be expected even then to conform fully to those foreign patterns which Western textbooks tend to interpret as the only rational ones. The similarity in executive techniques concerning accounting, budgeting, work scheduling, use of office machines, and inventory control will increase substantially, and so will the degree of objective technical efficiency in general. But the interpretations in each country or cultural area of family, government, competition, and risk as factors in business behavior will remain far more different, for right or wrong.

From another angle, public policy may attempt in an understanding way to bring Latin American management somewhat closer to the patterns from the North and West; but it will be well advised to expect only limited results from such an attempt. Foreign observers of Latin American management, at the same time, will be equally well advised to understand that there is more than one kind of "rational" management, and that there is a point on the human level beyond which the imitation of experiences from other cultures, no matter how successful there, becomes inefficient because communication and incentives prefer different channels.

Implications for Development Process

Management, Entrepreneurship, and Development Needs

These considerations apply especially to any expectation that the development process in Latin America will of necessity be based on entrepreneurship in the historical British or North American sense, and that the chief source of it will be the men presently in charge of private firms. Actually in Latin America as elsewhere the development process is affected both by the managers who show much entrepreneurship and those who do not; those who have much objective opportunity to show entrepreneurial initiative as owner-managers, senior partners, or uncontested heads of corporations, as well as those who face strong restraining influences from stockholders, family links, or a division of responsibilities within management. Presence of entrepreneurial initiative within the framework of managerial attitudes represents a highly significant trait of the latter but cannot be taken for granted in Latin America.[1]

There is no convincing evidence indicating that entrepreneurship, given certain conditions of technological, financial, and political organization, can or will develop *anywhere*. Initial accumulation of wealth may lead to dissipation through luxury consumption, to hoarding, or to usury just as easily as to productive or commercial initiative in the entrepreneurial sense. The prevailing value system in a community may either encourage or discourage innovation and individual initiative, or it may confine such opportunities to a socioeconomic and cultural elite to the

[1] Compare Heinz Hartmann, "Managers and Entrepreneurs: A Useful Distinction?" *Administrative Science Quarterly* (March, 1959); see also David McClelland, *op. cit.*, Chaps. 6–7; W. P. Strassmann, "The Industrialist," in John J. Johnson (ed.), *Continuity and Change in Latin America* (Stanford, Calif.: Stanford University Press, 1964).

exclusion of all the other groups, especially those of a tribal character. An Indian of the South American *altiplano*, for instance, has little hope ever to become an entrepreneur in the Western sense even within his own community, let alone the Peruvian or Ecuadorian economy as a whole.

An additional reservation suggests itself concerning the relationship between entrepreneurship and private ownership. In Western Europe and North America, the two concepts have been closely associated historically, although it was often the state which actually provided many of the conditions, incentives, and rewards of private entrepreneurship. Generally, it was assumed there that the entrepreneur was either identical with the private owner of a firm, or at least, was his direct representative. In contemporary Latin America such assumptions would be only partly true and sometimes not at all. The major initiative for economic innovation often comes from a government planning agency, and the planning officials and politicians assume much of the real risk that is involved in such initiative.

What then is the outlook for entrepreneurship in Latin America? Much has been written on ways to arouse an entrepreneurial spirit in areas of the world which somehow have never caught on in the past to a great drive for material progress through profit-minded, competitive, innovating, risk-taking enterprise.[2] To what extent is this a realistic way to regard the future outlook for the enterprise

[2] Bert F. Hoselitz, "Entrepreneurship and Economic Growth," in *Sociological Aspects of Economic Growth* (New York: Free Press of Glencoe, 1960). Bendix' interesting discussion, based on industrial history of England, the United States, and Russia, of a "change from entrepreneurial to managerial ideologies" seems to have very limited applications to Latin America thus far. Reinhard Bendix, *Work and Authority in Industry* (New York: John Wiley & Sons, 1956), especially Chaps. 1 and 4.

manager and the pattern of economic development in Latin America?

Of the elements just mentioned, only profit-mindedness is present there on any widespread scale, and even this concept requires substantial qualifications, as will be shown presently. To make much money promptly is undoubtedly a popular endeavor among enterprise managers and many other people, but this seldom means a drive for profit maximization through systematic productive effort or long-range planning. The necessity of an "industrial attitude" is frequently stressed but not easily adopted by those many who at heart are still merchants. Such attitudinal change is expected by the intellectual fringe to come from improving education, a hope which in the light of modern psychology appears to be only partly justified.

Entrepreneurship is not readily compatible with the expectation of a small market for any given product or enterprise, which we found to persist in large parts of Latin America. The typical attitude toward customers still assumes that the latter are quite limited in numbers and will remain so for the foreseeable future. This is especially true of countries with a "dual economy." As was shown in Chapter V, many enterprise managers have assumed traditionally that the majority of the population will never understand what modern industrial products are for, and will never have the cash to buy them. The new urban proletariat, the dwellers of shantytowns on the fringe of the larger cities, are not yet considered very seriously insofar as marketing possibilities are concerned.

Enterprise managers, therefore, tend to believe that high prices and profits are indispensable in dealing with that minority of the population that *is* able and interested to buy their goods. Aggregate demand is admittedly influenced by population growth but on the whole is judged to be so imperfectly elastic in the direction of expansion, at least, that price reductions and low profit per unit are considered ineffective, even dangerous, as they reduce the capital accumulation of enterprises and, with it, their ability to survive and expand. It is clear that such attitudes do not help the process of economic development.

For the same reason any large expenditure for advertising or any other drive for constant expansion of markets tends to be interpreted as a waste of effort and money. In fact, it might even make the consumers suspicious and might generally run afoul of unwritten codes of proper business behavior. This is also true of any ardent or "excessive" competition. As we saw in Chapter V, very often lip service is paid to the abstract principle of competition which is presented as an incentive for greater efficiency. When practiced in a specific field of business, however, competition is usually criticized as wasteful or inappropriate for a small economy, if not outright immoral. Admiration for the competitive results of North American or European industry is accompanied by polite regret that this lofty principle is unfortunately inapplicable to the poor country in question. The head of an important public finance institution in Northeast Brazil maintained, therefore, that private enterprise in that area had to be taught how to compete, especially through industrial production, and that his organization considered *generating* private entrepreneurship to be one of its decisive tasks.

The agrarian and family basis of enterprise management explains in part the traditional expectation of small markets, although a good many managers are willing to expand production if and when there has been *previous* evidence of expanding demand. An association of profit with market size often does not exist, or the profit urge itself assumes forms rather different from those in North America or Western Europe.

Profit and the Development Process

Even in advanced economies the role of the "profit motive" in guiding management or in stimulating economic development has often been overrated. There has also been insufficient clarity concerning the possible meanings of profit, especially the difference between short-range and long-range considerations and between making a profit (even a high one) and maximizing profit.[3]

The prevailing attitude toward profit in Latin America remains affected by the desire to get rich quick and then perhaps to retire early and to live happily—that is, idly— ever after. Here again things are beginning to change in certain areas which are past the initial stages of economic development. But at this point the extreme short-range view still predominates, especially in smaller firms, even when expansion is aimed at in a general way.

As pointed out in Chapters V and VII, a variety of reasons were offered in the interviews to explain the impossibility of long-range considerations in Latin America even when investment intentions exist in a general way. Inflation or, at least, inflationary experiences and dangers were often mentioned. Next to inflation, political instability— meaning anything from frequent change of ministers and development plans to social revolution—was cited frequently; one must make profit promptly while one's friends are still in the government. Others emphasized more

[3] See James K. Dent, "Organizational Correlates of the Goals of Business Management," *Journal of Personal Psychology*, Vol. 12, No. 3 (Autumn, 1959).

permanent or structural reasons such as the national character, chronic economic stagnation, or the dependence of the
country's chief export product on fluctuating world markets, and, perhaps, also on the vagaries of the climate.

Still others felt discouraged here again by the smallness
and vulnerability of the domestic market, or the extreme
difficulty in obtaining credit and capital for the enterprise
and the high and often discriminatory rates of interest. As a
result they saw a need for immediate huge profits as the
only possible source of investment. In other words, management was deemed to operate in an inadequate and
constantly changing environment. A leading Chilean
manager felt that the financial uncertainty during the mid-
fifties had its favorable side: If enterprise managers had
foreseen a mere fraction of the financial headaches they
were going to encounter, they would not have started any
new projects. It was only the uncertainty or ignorance
concerning the future which made them stick their neck
out in the short run, at least. A Brazilian manager commented, "You can *perhaps* plan here for twenty years
ahead, but not for one!"

Undoubtedly there is some truth in the reasons given for
the short-range approach, in a degree that varies according
to the developmental stage and economic condition of the
country. Yet there is also a good deal of rationalization in
such explanations of the prevailing concentration on the
short-range view, which clearly impedes a developmental
orientation of management. The reasons given are mostly
valid to some extent but not quite as valid or permanent as
they are claimed to be, and not always a convincing excuse
for waste, high prices, or failure to look for new customers.
The example of certain companies shows that it is not impossible to overcome the objective difficulties listed

through systematic action. Some of the managers who accepted these difficulties with resignation seemed quite content to have found a justification for living and managing their business on a day-to-day basis thus being spared the strain of long-range planning.

Profit expectations are influenced in Latin America in an incomparably greater degree than in advanced economies by nonmarket factors such as family status, political pull or instability, civil strife, social unrest, or the outlook for peace or war in the world. Uncertainty, far from meaning merely the objective impossibility of knowing or evaluating fully a competitive market situation or the trend of consumer preferences, involves the extreme difficulty of sizing up the effect of the weather on the next harvest in the absence of protection against floods, erosion, and plant diseases; the fluctuations of the world market for the major export product of the country; the probability of another clique or junta taking over the government by force, or the possibility that latent popular unrest may lead to riots and violence.

Similarly, risk refers in these countries not only to incompletely defined hazards in putting a new product on the market, for instance, but to the possibility that the total investment and assets of a firm or an individual, and perhaps his life, may be lost as a result of the possible fluctuations mentioned; a possibility, therefore, which it may be wiser to *avoid.* Confidence, under these conditions, means not merely an affirmative evaluation of the market prospects for specific kinds of goods or service, or even of the prospects of prosperity in a strictly economic sense, but an over-all picture of promising factors in the political, international, social, and economic outlook for the nation and area concerned. This is why there often is little public confidence in "paper," including not only money but company and government bonds.

The parameters of profit expectation, therefore, differ considerably here from those in more advanced economies. On the one hand, any rational drive for profit maximization would look like an impossible proposition since so many noneconomic as well as economic influences cannot be sized up or evaluated, let alone calculated with some degree of exactness. On the other hand, very high profit is considered indispensable precisely because of the great dangers involved in business activity and also because of the virtual impossibility of financing the growth of enterprises in any other way. The predominant aim, therefore, is very high profit without much concern for its maximization, and also the desire to achieve this profit quickly, without much thought to the more distant future and without any great predilection for systematic effort as the basis of profit.

For similar reasons, high productivity is more frequently admired than enforced, although this lag is beginning to shrink in a number of countries. Productivity is still thought of quite often as a luxury which only rich countries with a big market can afford—not as the basis of their wealth.

Such attitudes are enhanced by the frequent inadequacy of social overhead facilities in Latin American countries. When public arrangements and services such as water and power supply, transportation, housing, repair and market facilities cannot be counted on in a sufficient degree, the motivation for quick high profit (or, at least, the possibility of its public justification) increases. So does the objective need for resourcefulness of the management in providing some of these facilities on its own as the next best thing that can be done; but this does not necessarily mean that management is always aware of this need and ready to meet it.

Implications for Development Process

Why spend money and effort on the maintenance of equipment if future conditions are quite uncertain and risky in any case?

Entrepreneurship and Public Action

There are, of course, individual examples of genuine spontaneous entrepreneurship, sometimes represented through industrial investment companies. But they are too few and far between to encourage belief in an imminent upsurge of entrepreneurial mentality in Latin America. Moreover, training can create skilled managers more readily than entrepreneurs. The actual effectiveness and, especially, the constructive initiative of these managers will depend on their basic attitudes as individuals and as members of a definite social group.

Especially does this apply to their attitudes toward the development needs of their nation. Cooperation with the national development effort is increasingly expected in Latin America from the enterprise manager in our period by the other groups. But the investigation discussed in the preceding chapters indicates that such an attitude is only partly present now even though most people pay lip service to development. The differences are to some extent geographic; development-mindedness is more frequent and intensive among managers in Monterrey (Mexico), Cali (Colombia), and São Paulo (Brazil), for example, than it is among managers in other areas of the same countries or in some other nations. But there are additional variables according to the size of the firm, education and age of the manager, accustomed status of the family, and perhaps other factors. Investment and improvement intentions, it is true, are widespread and so is the corresponding urge to reinvest profits.

Stimulation of development through public action is often seen in terms of measures which would be of direct benefit to the firm or family group concerned, such as public credit and capital facilities for private enterprises. Education, public health and, in some cases, housing for the poor are also recognized as public functions as was shown in Chapter VI.

The prevailing attitudes toward tax reform and agrarian change differ. In both areas, especially that of taxation, reforms are rarely accepted readily yet and are not seen as essential for economic development, with the occasional exception of cases where they do not hurt the person and group concerned at all. Taxation is not often associated with development measures or any other useful purpose, and actual enforcement of taxes arouses resentment. More generally there is much jealousy, not always conscious, toward any implicit questioning by the state of the social leadership role of the business group and the families which it represents. Rationalization of private interests into national necessities is even more frequent in Latin America than in Europe or North America.

At the same time, development planning is widely seen by managers as legitimate function of the state. Public enterprises, however, are widely criticized; in Venezuela, for instance, some managers see them as a legacy of the Pérez dictatorship. In some countries, it is true, the public-enterprise manager with professional background and his private-enterprise colleague are not really different insofar as their general mentality is concerned, except for a less hostile attitude toward the existing type of government (but not toward political influences in management) on the part of the public-enterprise managers. In fact, professionally trained managers have been found readily interchangeable between private and public enterprises. It is only the relative of the owner, put into a managerial position, on the one side who differs substantially in his attitudes from the politician, put into a managerial position, on the other side. Even then the constant interaction of business, family, and politics within each major group tends to water down this latter difference.

The future pattern of the development process in Latin America is not, for all these reasons, likely to be based on an upsurge of entrepreneurial spirit as an autonomous and decisive force originating in the present management of enterprises. Certainly some examples of such a mentality and activity will continue to exist and they can even be stepped up to some extent through incentives and rewards. But essentially the pattern is more likely to be that of public utilization and stimulation of effective enterprise management as one important avenue toward the achievement of national development goals and plan objectives.

To judge from this investigation only a minority of Latin American managers relate their own activities to national development needs at this point. A much broader identification on their part with the national development effort would be required in order to fulfill the function described in the preceding paragraph. In particular, the frequent cleavage between the family goals of the enterprise —business expansion for prestige purposes and branching out into economically unrelated fields of business—on the one hand, and the needs of systematic economic development on the other, needs to be bridged or reduced. To what extent this will be possible beyond the examples already available remains to be seen. It is not impossible that the lack of communication with other social groups mentioned earlier expresses a basic cultural isolation from them that will persist for some time to come. In this case private-enterprise management might end up playing a less important role in the development process than its present *avant-garde* and its North American friends envision for it. This would be especially true if managers as a group should view the economic, political, and psychological costs of the social reforms and changes that development requires as exceeding the benefits that are likely to accrue to them from national economic development. It is too early to tell whether such an assumption will prevail in more than a few countries of Latin America, but the results of our investigation do not permit any definite conclusion to the contrary.

One might argue that in any case economic development policy in Latin America must make the best of the given situation even when the latter does not correspond to the preferences of Western economists, and that the net progress of areas such as São Paulo, Antioquia, or Monterrey has shown the ways in which the national development effort can utilize successful enterprise management (and vice versa). One could even go one step further and apply Albert O. Hirschman's theory of unbalanced growth to the spotty management situation in Latin America, thus expecting precisely a few available cases of efficient enterprise management there to act as stimulus both for the rise of others and for positive public action. The latter, in any case, will continue to play a much greater part in the development process there than it has historically in Western Europe or North America where reliance on private profit has prevailed.

In other words, despite the objective needs mentioned earlier, the whole idea that management, either private or public, must essentially rely on its own ingenuity and initiative as measured by yields, rather than being supported if not subsidized from above is still fairly rare in Latin America, though it has been making headway in recent years. This limitation has definite implications for the economic role of the state as perceived by enterprise managers in this area. In the light of this discussion and the findings indicated in Chapter VI, what is the future role of governmental development activity in the Latin American countries in relation to the role of enterprise management?

As we have seen, managers mostly approve of public development planning or coordination. In many areas they even accept public enterprises as long as they are confined to fields which private business cannot handle as too costly, too risky, or nonprofitable, and as long as they avoid competition with private companies. Among other social and ideological groups there has been much disappointment with the conduct both of public and private enterprises, along with advocacy of maintenance, perhaps expansion, of the public sector but also of its concentration on *new* industries or productive facilities.

The two principles—public development planning along with avoidance of competition of public enterprises with private business—are not irreconcilable once they have been clearly defined. It is precisely the lack of definition of economic policy goals for the future on the part of the government, which private managers in Venezuela, in particular, complained about. As long as one side sees exploitation in any profitable business while the other side sees communism in any public intervention, there is little room for an understanding or division of labor. There are indications, however, that the underlying attitudes have begun to change.

On the side of private management, such incipient change would seem to be indicated by the growing concern of businessmen and organizations with their social responsibilities. The Asociación Venezolana de Ejecutivos, the Unión Social de Empresarios Católicos in Chile, and other groups in various countries have raised related problems in their meetings and publications. Such discussions have sometimes touched upon the problem of relating economic criteria to other basic values in life, especially the religious norms which are of such importance in the Latin American tradition.

At this point it certainly cannot be said that the problem has been resolved. Rationalizations and self-deception continue to occur. Endeavors to define and implement clearly the social responsibilities of private enterprise in the development process have thus far been hampered in Latin America by two kinds of limitations.

First, businessmen have tended to interpret "social responsibility" in a praiseworthy but narrow (and sometimes fearful) way as medical and welfare facilities and perhaps company-owned housing for the workers of a firm, or else as a right and duty to take the conduct of society into their hands through appropriate organization as a group.

Second, some of them have vainly tried to combine such approaches with a "neoliberal" hostility toward any economic action on the part of public authorities, a hostility based on basic confusion between private ownership and individual initiative or a free market. "Social responsibility" of private enterprise thus became a mere negative attempt to ward off competing public action, rather than the expression of profound attitudinal change. Possible conflicts between self-interest and social responsibility, or between economic and religious norms of behavior, were then "resolved" by rationalizations. Economic action by public authorities was recognized as valid by this group only when they acted strictly as servants of private enterprise, for example, by developing local industries or power plants out of public money, then selling them to private groups at a bargain rate.

One of the most impressive needs that emerges from our investigation thus concerns the strengthening of the development orientation and, more generally, of thinking in terms of national economic necessities among private managers in Latin America and, particularly, among their business associations. Examples of development-mindedness in individual managers can certainly be found, especially among the younger generation of executives, but they are still fairly rare. Possibly greater use of social economists who could constantly interpret development needs to enterprise managers would be helpful.

Cooperation on the part of private enterprise with the public development policy in decisions on investment, prices, wages, imports and exports, and other matters is the decisive yardstick of social responsibility, far more so than social services in the plant with all due respect for such services when they are not merely instituted out of fear of radicalism or as a matter of public relations. Social responsibility, in other words, needs to be interpreted by Latin American managers as the integration of individual enterprise decisions on investment, plant expansion, or dividends, into the national development effort. It is admittedly a more difficult and challenging task to build social responsibility right into the decision-making of the firm than to have the latter make profit in any available way and then to channel some fraction of it into a maternity ward or playground.

Cooperation, of course, is a two-way road. Public authorities in charge of a development program must make a conscious effort to reach the mind of the enterprise managers. They must also offer them concrete suggestions, assistance, and incentives for behavior that supports the objectives of the program. Such behavior can especially be encouraged by removing indecision and instability in public administration, which have often impeded the development process in Latin American countries.

"Economic" development actually represents a combination of social, psychological, political, and financial processes which all partly presuppose and partly generate an attitudinal change in important economic groups—in this case the enterprise managers. For many managers in Latin America it is still a new experience to think in terms of what *they* can contribute to development planning and its implementation, not merely in terms of what they and their firms will get out of a national development that will somehow come about through other people's effort. Conversely, Latin American governments and their development planning agencies need to examine constantly the ways in which they can contribute, by providing training facilities and through other means, to an efficient enterprise management which is well adapted to the local needs and cultural traits of the population concerned. Last but not least, the government, the development agencies, and the political organisms must give the managerial group the feeling that they are untainted by corruption or favoritism. The policy implications of the preceding discussion will be further examined in the last chapter.

Politics, Development, and Enterprise

In Chapter I we discussed the typical ways in which business, family life, and politics are intertwined in the Latin American nations with their legacy of feudalism, slavery, colonialism, or militarism. Against this background any expectation of a government-free economy holds little promise there for the foreseeable future. The real and decisive issue both for enterprise managers and for development is *what kind* of government is to preside over the coming socioeconomic changes.

Is it to be based on a system of "pull" under which a private firm can get import licenses, tax benefits, or other favors only if its head knows the right people and perhaps is related to them? Does government represent one big corruption machine where acceptance of bribes is internalized in the mind of each official and constitutes his real source of income from which he is expected to supply kickbacks to those above him? Has he got an extra job or two outside the government so that he only shows up in his office for brief visits at uncertain hours? Is the job itself based on any legitimate function or does it represent make-work that needs to be "justified" by some pseudoactivity, perhaps the ingenious invention of complications for businessmen and other citizens in their daily lives?

Or is the government machinery reasonably honest, objective, and efficient? Only anarchism in the guise of laissez faire would deny that government can ever have such qualities. Actually there are some such examples— admittedly not very many—from newly developing areas including Latin America. There are also, for that matter, examples of nepotism and corruption in more advanced economies. There is no law of nature that would make this problem insoluble, but it does need to be solved before either enterprise management or the development process can function satisfactorily, no matter how sound may be the abstract principles of both.

Even where government practices are reasonably honest

and objective and where genuine civil service exists, enterprise management as well as development measures may be held up time and again by exasperating fluctuations in the composition and economic policy of governments. An investment decision may face insoluble uncertainty if previous experience indicates that the present Minister of Finance with his entire monetary and fiscal program may be gone in a few months and that an entirely new policy may follow, only to be overthrown itself a little later. This has been true even of countries which have not been plagued by military coups and competing juntas.

This problem overlaps with that of political parties in Latin America. In a few countries, permanent parties with a definite ideology or program compete democratically for the support of the voters. More often, however, a "party" represents the personal support of a strong leader and is conducive to volatile, whimsical, and socially irresponsible types of political organization, conquest and maintenance of power, and economic policy if any. An enterprise may profit from such happenings for awhile if its ruling family is closely connected with the political group at the top, but may lose far more when this group is succeeded by another. Development policy suffers even more from the prevalence of unmitigated power motives and economic vagaries that usually characterize this kind of political structure.

Actually it takes a political system of a rather sophisticated and responsible nature to carry through effectively the kind of development planning that is needed in newly developing areas. Development planning in such areas, with the exception of Communist regimes, usually includes a number of important targets that are to be reached through appropriate governmental stimulation of private enterprise.

Implications for Development Process

To the extent that this aim cannot be achieved—for example, if the capital needs concerned are very large or if private initiative and managerial training are lagging—these stimuli are supplemented by the direct establishment and operation of some enterprises by the state, or by government financing of privately managed firms. In the enterprises of the public sector the crucial difference is that between autonomous, professional management on the one hand and bureaucratic or political administration on the other. In any case the kind of mixed-enterprise system that characterizes newly developing nations stands or falls with the nature of the underlying processes in government and politics.

The Role of Foreign Investment and Aid

In the light of the managerial attitudes described toward development, government, and politics, what is the outlook for ready reception and a fruitful development role of foreign investment and aid in Latin America?

In the first place, if private managers there are not unqualifiedly happy about foreign investment, as was pointed out in Chapter VII, no other population group is likely to be. Any expectation that large-scale foreign investment will be the mainstay of Latin American development, or a major effect of economic integration, would therefore be unrealistic. At any rate, only those who see underdevelopment purely as a matter of capital shortage could place their main hope in a great inflow of capital from abroad. But capital shortage in less developed areas has been due in a large degree to the outflow of funds actually formed in these areas or to inefficient use of existing funds at home. More important, even genuine capital shortage is only one of the major shortcomings there, the others being lack of both general and specialized education and know-how, inadequate power supply and communications, mass diseases, and inefficient public administration.

Unless these shortcomings are remedied, capital inflow will often do more good to the foreign investors than to the receiving economy. Moreover, even if the economic blessings of foreign investment were completely unmixed it would still be up against rising nationalism sooner or later and would, in fact, contribute to such rise through its mere presence. A strong foreign element, perhaps amounting to foreign control of the decisive resources in a newly developing nation with strong urge for economic as well as political independence, easily becomes emotionally intolerable. This is true even if the behavior of foreign investors should be faultlessly tactful and understanding, and if their way of looking at foreign investment in Latin America in particular were much closer to that of enterprise managers and other groups there than it actually is.

This is not a general argument against foreign investment in Latin America or other developing areas, but it is an argument against placing any excessive hopes on it either from the foreign or the national point of view. Greater hope would seem to rest, first, in joint business ventures and, second, in private technical assistance. A combination of these two principles is even better. Foreign capital which joins forces with domestic investors and supplies the enterprise not only with funds but with extensive technical assistance will have the best prospects. The foreign element in the management of such an enterprise will chiefly consist of high-level technicians and some participation in the general supervision, and will be expected to diminish gradually after the initial phase of the enterprise. The future of wholly foreign-owned firms, branches, and subsidiaries looks far less promising for the reasons mentioned earlier.

What about foreign aid? As we have seen, any expectations that outside funds will more or less finance domestic development have begun to disappear among Latin American enterprise managers and presumably other groups, too. For the more developed countries it is time to recognize that economic development does not merely depend on funds available, that it cannot be financed from the outside in any decisive degree, that it does not automatically remove communism, and that such motivation diminishes the moral impact of both development and aid.

Related qualifications have affected the Alliance for Progress, too. A relatively favorable reception has been given to the basic idea despite serious doubts about its effectiveness on the practical level. The conclusion suggests itself that the Alliance should present itself more clearly as a mutual inter-American commitment, and that the assistance involved should be unmistakably earmarked for development purposes only. Moreover, inter-American technical assistance and the channeling of loan funds for private and public purposes through development banks could have been more strongly emphasized from the outset.

As for the reform requirements of the Alliance, there has been little evidence thus far that the upper strata of Latin American societies are really ready in the emotional, economic, or political sense to go ahead with land reform and tax reform. There is in fact only very limited evidence, in the history of upper classes, of a voluntary enactment of inevitable reforms early enough to forestall more troublesome alternatives.

Enterprise managers or, for that matter, "business" in Latin America are too new and fluid a group to be frozen into rigid classes and cannot always be characterized as

IX

Conclusions

OUR investigation of managerial attitudes toward economic development in Latin America has indicated that these attitudes cannot simply be expected to duplicate sooner or later the mentality of managers in more advanced economies, not even all of its traits during the period when these latter economies according to more recent terminology were still underdeveloped. We have also found indications that certain policies of the Latin American nations themselves, with supporting measures of the developed nations and international organs, can influence the attitudes of Latin American management in a direction which brings it closer to the requirements of socioeconomic development. This concluding chapter attempts to point up the possibilities and limitations of enterprise management in Latin America as a factor in the development process.

The difference between the general setting there and that of North American and Western European management can be summed up as follows:

1. The mere fact that in a *technical* sense management does not need to develop anew in each country and that it can adjust the historical experiences of others to local needs, potentially speeds up its knowledge and processes. At the same time, unnecessary or premature destruction of older patterns of economic organization when the population is not ready for management in the Western sense may arouse resistance, thus slowing down the developmental processes it was meant to speed up.

2. The evidence discussed in Chapter II indicates that the application of the historical experiences of others in encouraging systematic management is limited and circumscribed by the cultural setting as well as the developmental stage of each country. The very concept of management and its concrete manifestations will differ even though terminology and techniques may be imported from a country with greater managerial experience.

3. There cannot be, therefore, a body of general rules for public policy on management, which would be applicable without substantial adjustments in every country and development phase. Many training techniques, it is true— for example, instruction in the use of business machines— have wide international applications. But this in itself is not the essence of management, which consists in the organization and direction of specific kinds of people in their working processes.

4. Any rules of managerial behavior that are elaborated for a given country and culture should be applicable to the

managers of private, public, or cooperative enterprises with slight modifications according to the type of ownership. The borderline between ownership types in Latin America is not always clear-cut and mixed enterprises are frequent. Moreover, managers may shift from one type to another and the differences in attitude toward efficiency and labor, and above all toward the general development needs of the country concerned, do not necessarily follow the division lines of ownership systems.

It is possible, however, to suggest a number of principles that might guide public administrators in most countries in their endeavor to include systematically the managerial groups in the development effort.

In the first place, the makers of development policies in Latin America and elsewhere need to understand the distinction between management and entrepreneurship, and the fact that the latter is not confined to, or excluded from, any particular form of ownership. The essential ingredient is readiness to assume responsibility and risk, and active interest in innovation and change for the better. Managers in any ownership type of enterprise—private, public, or cooperative—*can* show such spirit and translate it into action. Financial as well as nonfinancial benefits can be used in order to reward such behavior or to influence the national scale of values in this direction by making clear that such behavior is desirable in the public interest.

Some degree of transition to professional management can be expected in the course of economic development as was shown in Chapter III. The family enterprise clearly cannot be done away with overnight anywhere in Latin America, nor is it necessarily bad or incompatible with professional management. As economic development proceeds, however, family connections or prestige will increasingly be considered a suitable basis of managerial selection only when those selected also have the training, knowledge, and mentality required to be an effective manager under the cultural and socioeconomic conditions of the country concerned. Needless to say, a government which itself is based on nepotism will have a hard time persuading management to carry out more lofty principles of selection and action. The managerial role in economic development, therefore, like many other policies depends in a large degree on the existence or establishment of the appropriate kind of government.

General public policy with regard to enterprise management should aim, with realistic allowance for cultural and historical differences, at a lessened reliance of management on family links and political pull, and greater reliance on systematic training and specialized knowledge of production, markets, and work organization in the industry concerned. Encouragement of these principles will reduce in due course the authoritarian improvisation habits in management and will correspondingly increase in larger enterprises, at least, the delegation of responsibilities, division of labor, clear definition of functions among executives, and flexibility within the organizational structure. At the same time, public policy should also be based on the principle of making the economic efficiency and social utility of the enterprise in the development process a decisive guidepost of managerial action. For much the same reasons, prestige considerations need to be toned down in policy decisions about the stimulation and location of early industries within an essentially agricultural economy. The training of farm managers and the general interpretation of agriculture and those industries that are based on it as promising features of the development process are of great importance. Not only showmanship in building jet airports, for instance, where country roads are more urgent and stimulating, but neglect of managerial training compared with the construction of shiny factory buildings, should be avoided in almost any country. This is not meant to be an argument against the stimulating effects of certain types of unbalanced growth.[1]

Another principle which our investigation suggests for public policy in Latin America aims at persuading enterprise managers that the traditional limitations of production and distribution in an underdeveloped economy do not necessarily last forever. This applies especially to conscious or unconscious assumptions about an inevitably small market in the nation concerned or about a dual economy which permanently excludes large sectors of the population from the national market. It also applies to corresponding neglect of a drive for higher productivity, lower prices, and increased consumer satisfaction in general. Likewise, the attitude that competition represents a luxury which a less developed economy can never afford, invites counteraction not only among the managers of private firms but among their colleagues in public enterprises as well. For even in monopolistic state enterprises there is much room for competition in performance among departments and individuals.

It is equally important to stimulate long-range planning in the management of enterprises and to discourage the association of managerial activity with the drive for immediate profit or "getting rich quick." This stimulation can be carried out, as some available examples show, through coordination of social services such as road building and

[1] Albert O. Hirschman, *The Strategy of Economic Development* (New Haven, Conn.: Yale University Press, 1958).

housing with long-range investment plans of individual enterprises. Other methods include public capital supply for private long-range investment that is integrated into the development program and, of course, a more general policy of stability in monetary and industrial relations. Such an endeavor to build up an atmosphere of confidence in economic society can well be combined with an attempt to make enterprise managers understand that they cannot carry out their function without taking some calculated risks all the time.

The financial attitudes of managers can be influenced by public action in such a way that real shortages of capital are not compounded by wasteful use of available capital, and that the formation and productive use of capital are encouraged. This is a field for incentive taxation as well as public policies for long-term credit and capital supply. Such measures, it is true, may be ineffective if they follow prolonged inflationary experiences or if there are perceived dangers of inflation. On the other hand, it must be made clear that fear of inflation is not an excuse for lack of long-range planning or for inefficient use of capital in either private or public enterprises.

The financial attitudes of each manager, in Latin America as elsewhere, are greatly influenced also by his personal traits, and the general impact of personality on managerial effectiveness is enormous. The possibilities for public action in this respect look rather limited, however. The incidence of specific personalities depends far more on the cultural and socioeconomic setting of the past than on present public policy. Certain cultures discourage the emergence of strong, active personalities or their successful application in management. Public policy, it is true, can reward such personalities for actual performance through an array of possible measures which may range from cash to decorations. But the most effective reward in more than one culture is personal satisfaction with the job done. Public policy can contribute to it by expressing its recognition as well.

In the relations between management and labor, the exploitative or paternalist attitudes of managers, which have been so frequent in Latin America, can be consciously discouraged by public policy. Social legislation is one way to express and institutionalize such discouragement. At the same time, both moral and financial incentives to workers and peasants, as well as managers, for higher productivity should be provided. The casual work habits of many of the poorer populations cannot be changed overnight, and no such attempt will be promising if it clashes head on with established cultural values. Yet gradual change in these values is not impossible. What matters most is to make all the classes understand the meaning and possibility of higher productivity and the benefits that may accrue from it to themselves.

Such an attempt will be most likely to succeed if it is carried out by a government which enjoys the confidence of the major population groups and the intellectuals, and which gives all of these groups the feeling that it is concerned with *their* welfare, not just that of the rich or of foreign powers. Social radicalism needs to be channeled into productive attitudes and into support for a national development program, away from either blind hatred or servile glorification of other nations and regimes.

As for foreign investment, there is need for the governments and nations of Latin America to decide what they really want. They cannot go on crying for foreign capital and then yell "imperialism" when it comes. It is illogical to attract it one day and nationalize it the next or interpret such practices of other countries in the process of development as the wave of the future. If they think that foreign investment is prejudicial to their national independence, the logical conclusion is to do without foreign investment and to state this decision in unmistakable terms. Such candor on the part of public authorities will encourage a comparable realism among the managers of domestic enterprises toward any possibilities of foreign capital participation.

Managers of foreign-owned or foreign-controlled enterprises, at the same time, must also beware of economic schizophrenia. If they are foreigners, they should realize that they cannot expect to live and work in another country forever without adjusting themselves to it sooner or later. Unless they come just for a short while as technical advisers, they should make up their mind within, say, two or three years whether they want to stay there for good and become citizens of their new country, or whether they prefer to return to the old country. They cannot expect to occupy a managing position forever and yet to remain strangers in the country where they live. This should be made clear to them soon after they arrive, or preferably before.

This consideration also applies to the owners of the foreign capital invested. The foreign investor should understand that no country in our period is likely to let others own a large part of its economy permanently. Public policy should clearly decide whether it wishes to try for foreign loans without any managerial responsibility on the part of the lenders; straight portfolio investment for a limited space of time; equity investment with or without managerial participation, which is essentially meant to remain in the country including the profits it yields; joint international business ventures with joint management, or any other form.

One thing is clear from our investigation and from the Latin American postwar experience in general: foreign investment on the old lines, with constant export of the profits and perhaps with permanent foreign management which never thinks of integrating itself into national life, has increasingly poor prospects in most of Latin America for political and psychological reasons, no matter what might be its purely economic merits.

At the same time, the rapidly rising nationalism in Latin American nations is often fanned by perception of their headaches even by enterprise managers, let alone other groups, as purely national. This nationalism needs to be channeled through conscious public action away from aggressive-destructive forms and "anti-imperialism" or other strong emotions into a systematic effort for constructive development planning. In this endeavor, public policy should supply a flow of reliable economic data. It should also determine the specific forms in which the collaboration of managerial groups in this planning is to be enlisted. The already predominant view of these groups that governmental coordination of economic development is necessary can be utilized in order to induce them to collaborate systematically with the development program.

Such collaboration will be effective only if the government itself is respected and trusted by most people. Even financial or other incentives for management will be interpreted as mere handouts if this is what people generally expect from their existing government. In order to yield the desired economic effects, any public policy designed to encourage a spirit of responsibility, innovation, and productivity in private or public managers presupposes a free, honest, consistent, and efficient government.

At the same time, a government of this kind cannot afford to disregard the question of existing and desired attitudes of both private and public managers under given conditions of culture and history. For these attitudes can constitute a very important aspect of a general program for economic development. Success in the incorporation of the emerging managerial groups into the development effort of newly developing countries can also have an important feedback effect upon enterprise management in more advanced economies whose management and business have been exposed to many international uncertainties about the future of the social order.

The policy implications of the preceding findings and considerations are summed up in the two concluding sections.

Policy Implications for Latin America

The available evidence strongly suggests that the development process in most of Latin America will be based on the incorporation of private management and initiative into the public development goals, with subsidiary aid from foreign sources. It would be unrealistic there to wait for an autonomous rise of entrepreneurship on a large scale, to rely on a central planning based exclusively on public ownership, or to set the main hope in a massive flow of foreign capital, aid, or know-how. *All* of these elements are, and in all probability will continue to be, present in some degree in the development process of Latin American countries, but none of them in isolation can be expected to serve as sufficient basis for large-scale development.

With due allowance for differences in national and cultural conditions, the following aims and policies for Latin American nations with regard to enterprise management suggest themselves in general in the interest of a more effective development process:

1. The training of professional managers who can run either publicly or privately owned enterprises should be stepped up. In this training process, emphasis should be placed not only on sound knowledge of plant organization, accounting, inventory control, and other technical procedures in general but on their interpretation and adaptation in terms of the specific background and needs of the country and population groups concerned.

2. In a broader sense the encouragement of development-mindedness and awareness of national economic needs and of international factors in the development of the nation concerned should occupy an equally prominent role in the training of the new managerial groups. As we have seen, there is also urgent need in most areas of Latin America for improved communication between management and other social groups such as organized labor, small landowners, and university students. Such communication will help managers to obtain a clearer picture of the possibilities and limitations of their own social role in comparison with that of other groups. This will also help remove certain cleavages and contradictions in the managers' mind between their perception of the outside world and the reality of social life.

3. There is room for certain incentives designed to broaden the ownership basis of private corporations, especially a suitable tax policy. But it should not be assumed that this enterprise form will ever find as wide an application

in Latin American countries as it has in North America or Western Europe.

4. Expansion ambitions of enterprises should be encouraged to the extent that they are based on realistic appraisal of the capital supply available and of factual and potential consumer markets, on readiness to reinvest profits extensively even when some risk is involved, and on the contribution of such expansion to national development goals. *Fomento* loans and tax benefits can be used for such guidance. Transition from nominal to functional stock markets and increase of facilities for the flotation of corporate bonds abroad offer some additional possibilities for the financing of future expansion.

5. Encouragement of a reflux of Latin American capital from North America and Western Europe is of fundamental importance. The essential precondition for actual success of such a policy is political stability and a fair and efficient administration.[2]

6. Clear-cut delineation of the intended roles of the government and private enterprise, respectively, in the course of economic development is of great significance. Such delineation was mentioned in the interviews with great frequency as a basic condition for an effective social contribution of private enterprise management.

7. There is need for a definition of the intended role of public enterprises, their concentration on those economic fields which private firms cannot be expected to cover effectively, and expert, efficient, and honest administration of the public enterprises. The latter should be interpreted

[2] See the papers by Daniel Cosío Villegas and Herbert Emmerich in E. De Vries and J. Medina E. (eds.), *Social Aspects of Economic Development in Latin America*, Vol. I (Paris: Unesco, 1963).

both by private management and the development planners as a valid and essential sector of national development activities under Latin American conditions, not as a mere drag on the private sector, a device to absorb its unprofitable segments, or an outlet for political sinecure.

8. There should be at the same time due consideration, within the public infrastructure activities, of the basic needs of those private enterprises, especially new ones, which are counted on as part of the development process. In particular, sufficient technical assistance and information facilities of the government are needed to help in the initial stages of new enterprises; so also are tax incentives and capital aid from public development banks.

9. Representatives of enterprise management should be incorporated into the process of development planning itself, along with the previously mentioned assignment of specific development tasks to the private sector and use of appropriate incentives in this direction. This, indeed, presupposes a far stronger development orientation of the latter than has thus far been in existence in many areas of Latin America.

10. There is need for an effective land policy which is centered not merely on changes in land use, tenure, and technology but on the incorporation of the *campesino* into the national markets. This certainly requires public credit, price, welfare, education, health, transport, and electrification policies especially designed to lift the rural population out of its traditional isolation and apathy; but it also presupposes, on the part of enterprise managers, greatly increased awareness of the potential role and contribution of the *campesino* in the national consumer markets and productivity levels of the future.

Last but not least, all the socioeconomic groups should

Conclusions

abandon any semantic dogmatism that tends to obscure the real practical issues, and should help in concentrating the general development effort on the most promising combination of public and private initiative toward the national development goals.[3]

Policy Implications for the United States

Insofar as United States policies toward the Latin American development processes and needs are concerned, realism is again the most urgent requirement. Preaching an abstract free-enterprise doctrine over and over again will not do. The need for realism applies specifically to that

---

[3] Compare the following passages from "Declaration of Economic Policy of the National Government," *News of Venezuela*, Central Office of Coordination and Planning, Caracas (June, 1963), pp. 10ff.:

> The good functioning of a mixed economy, like Venezuela's, demands that the economic policy be drawn up in an integral manner, in clear terms, and that it be carried out in a coherent and decided way. Once the scope of the State's managerial action in the economy is known, private enterprise is placed in the position to move with greater security. Thus, cooperation and complementation between public and private sectors must be brought about in order to accelerate the economic development.
>
> In general, the Government limits the managerial action of the State fundamentally to those activities:
>
> (a) which, as public services (e.g., railroads, telecommunications, electricity and gas) naturally pertain to its sphere of action; and
>
> (b) which, as basic industries, require large investments and are suppliers of essential raw materials to a large number of other industries thus exerting a powerful influence over the whole economy.
>
> Enterprises of the State or mixed enterprises, as those of private capital, should be conducted according to the principles of a sound and efficient management. Consequently, the functioning of the former will be kept under revision so that they would achieve, in the shortest possible time, a high level of financial self-sufficiency.

crucial problem of newly developing areas, the relationship between their private and public sectors. The black-and-white thinking on this subject that has been so frequent among North American managers and their business associations is sometimes imitated in Latin America but has long been at odds with the economic facts even in the United States. On the practical level, specific demands from business sources for defense contracts, tariffs, subsidies, credit guarantees, highway construction, and other government influences in economic life have been continuous there even while abstract criticism of government spending and intervention has gone on relentlessly. Quite often American business managers have preached to Latin Americans the evils of government and the virtues of Free Enterprise—the latter usually associated with private ownership no matter how subsidized or restrictive—while failing to notice that they were not practicing these theoretical principles in their own backyard and, in fact, *expected* government intervention on a large scale. The underlying psychological mechanism of semantic self-deception has been discussed repeatedly.[4]

Neither will a United States policy of handouts on the spur of the moment to anyone who claims or is deemed to be threatened by communism be sufficient. The time is also past for any dollar diplomacy whose prime objective was to open up opportunities for profitable U.S. investment in Latin America and then to protect this investment without regard to political and ideological consequences either there or in the rest of the world.

Positive measures which suggest themselves in the light of this investigation, especially of the attitudes of Latin

[4] For instance, F. X. Sutton *et al.*, *The American Business Creed* (Cambridge, Mass.: Harvard University Press, 1956).

American enterprise managers toward foreign investment and aid, are therefore the following:

1. Direct private investment of U.S. capital in Latin America, preferably coupled with technical assistance, should expect encouragement only in those cases in which the investors are prepared (a) to leave the capital invested including the bulk of the profits indefinitely in the country concerned, (b) to have high-level representatives of the investing group move to Latin America permanently, (c) to incorporate their investment into the current development programs or aims of the nations concerned, (d) to renounce any claim to special privileges or to protection of their investment by the U.S. Government, even in case of nationalization, (e) to join forces with investors and executive personnel from the country concerned, and (f) to use scrupulously fair methods of competition toward weaker native enterprises.

2. United States private loans to Latin American enterprises, both private and public, accompanied by technical assistance, should be encouraged insofar as they meet the applicable requirements listed above. Private technical assistance to Latin American enterprises on a fee basis also deserves stimulation.

3. Future prospects for wholly owned branches or majority ownership of firms in Latin America by U.S. companies are dubious and no particular encouragement of such arrangements can be recommended. New foreign activities in the extractive industries also have doubtful prospects.

4. Training programs for Latin American management personnel, with the participation of U.S. instructors, can be valuable if the curriculum, study materials, and instructors' attitudes are in line with the specific requirements of Latin American development needs, and if any ethnocentric imi-

tation of U.S. experiences, procedures, or preconceptions is avoided.

5. The Alliance for Progress, or any comparable aid program that may follow it up, should be interpreted as a program of cooperation between the United States and the Latin American nations themselves for the sole purpose of fostering the socioeconomic development of the latter in specific ways, with emphasis on technical assistance—not as a unilateral handout, political aid against radical threats, propaganda for an abstract free-enterprise system, or entering wedge for a huge flow of foreign capital in search of easy profits.

6. United States attitudes toward Latin American governments should avoid the extremes of uncritical support for dictators who profess anticommunism, and refusal of aid to public enterprises or development plans. Considerations of administrative efficiency and public confidence in granting development aid to a government are unavoidable, but development planning including long-range agrarian and tax reforms and a combination of public and private initiative on the basis of political freedom should be considered the most hopeful arrangement.

7. Aid for development or any other purpose should not be imposed on any Latin American government or made contingent upon political support of the U.S. foreign policy of the moment. Moreover, U.S. development aid should present itself from the outset as a transitory device for a limited number of years determined in advance and it should be channeled in a large degree through the United Nations, the Organization of American States, and their specialized agencies.

8. Study and encouragement of opportunities for inter-American investment is of great importance, especially

with a view to the possibilities of a Common Market and the diversification of economies traditionally depending on one export product.

9. Realistic appraisal of the strength of forces favoring national, and sometimes nationalized, ownership of basic resources in many Latin American countries is indispensable. This includes consideration on the part of foreign investors of the possibility of investing in a new enterprise for a specified number of years, after which the enterprise would become national property, with appropriate compensation arrangements made in advance.

* * *

Enactment of the policies recommended in the two preceding sections may not suffice to integrate Latin American enterprise management completely with the economic development aims of each nation and of the entire region. But it will bring these two endeavors far closer to such integration than they were found to be in the course of this study.

APPENDIXES

APPENDIX 1

Questionnaire

1. Who owns this enterprise and what connection do the managers have with the owners?
2. How would you describe the chief aim that guides the management of this company?
3. What are the criteria of this company in selecting and promoting executive personnel?
4. To what extent do you consider efficient management a matter of training?
   (a) What kind of training?
5. Do you have a present intention to invest more money in the enterprise? (If yes) From what sources?
   (a) Are you affected by any shortage of capital or credit?
   (b) Do you expect immediate profit from new investment?
   (c) To what extent are you prepared to take risks?
6. What are the chief satisfactions which you find in managerial activity?

(a) Are there any dissatisfactions?

7. Has the level of productivity in this enterprise increased in recent years or not?

    (a) How do the workers react to measures for higher productivity?

8. Do you think this country in general is well on its way toward a developed economy or not?

9. Has inflation been of benefit to your company or not?

    (a) Has inflation encouraged economic development or not?

10. What do you think is the most pressing need of this country in order to stimulate development?

11. Do you think that people in this country show any special traits which affect business and development or not?

12. What do you consider the proper role of the state in economic development?

13. What do you think is the future of foreign investment in this country from its own point of view?

    (a) Which form of foreign investment do you consider the best?

14. Do you think there is still need for foreign development aid here?

    (a) What about the Alliance for Progress?

15. What do you think the economy of this country will be like in 25 years or so?

    (a) What about a Latin American Common Market?

16. Is there anything else of importance you would like to say about the development problems of this country?

APPENDIX 2

Location of Interviews

Country	Areas
Chile	Santiago, Valparaíso, Concepcíon, Temuco, Valdivia, Osorno, Puerto Montt, Punta Arenas
Colombia	Bogotá, Medellín, Cali
Peru	Lima, Cuzco
Bolivia	La Paz
Argentina	Buenos Aires, Mendoza
Paraguay	Asuncíon
Uruguay	Montevideo
Brazil	Pôrto Alegre, São Paulo, Rio de Janeiro, Belo Horizonte, Salvador, Recife, Fortaleza
Mexico	Mexico City, Guadalajara, Monterrey
Guatemala	Guatemala City
El Salvador	San Salvador
Venezuela	Caracas, Maracay, Valencia

Distribution of Interviews by Country, Industry, and Ownership

Country	Industrial Enterprises								
	Textiles, Clothing, Footwear	Metal Products	Electric Products	Chemicals and Fuel	Foodstuffs, Tobacco	Other or Varied	Total Industrial	Finance and Insurance	Commerce
Chile ᶜ	15	18	3	9	7	11	63	7	11
Colombia	1				4	4	9	5	
Peru		1			2		3	2	3
Bolivia									1
Argentina	1	1		2	1	1	6		3
Uruguay	2				1		3	3	2
Paraguay									1
Brazil	6	6		2	12	9	35	6	8
Mexico	4	6	1	5	11	7	34	8	6
Guatemala	2	1		3	4	1	11	1	3
El Salvador	1			2	1	1	5	2	3
Venezuela	2	5		4	6	7	24	6	2
Totals	34	38	4	27	49	41	193	40	43

ᵃ "Others" include government officials, economists, and productivity experts with experience in the field of this study.

ᵇ Including one cooperative enterprise.

ᶜ The figures for Chile include reinterviews in 1963.

| Nonindustrial Enterprises | | | | | | Managers | | Others [a] | Total |
Transportation	Construction	Mining	Agriculture	Other or Varied	Total nonindustrial	Private	Public		
5	5	4	6	1	39	95	7	12	114
	1			1	7	14	2	4	20
			1		6	8	1	3	12
		1			2	2			2
				1	4	10		3	13
			2		7	10		1	11
					1	1		1	2
2					16	49	2	26	77
	3	3		4	24	52	6 [b]	15	73
			3	3	10	21		4	25
			1	1	7	12		3	15
					8	31	1	7	39
7	8	9	12	12	131	305	19	79	403

Index

Index

Development needs (*continued*)
35, 44, 47, 50, 69, 71, 79ff., 92,
112ff., 127, 141, 143ff., 152, 155,
163ff., 169, 180, 187
De Vries, E., 189

Ecuador, 4, 156
Education, 23, 31, 36, 45, 52, 64f.,
79, 88f., 105, 129, 174, 176, 181
El Salvador, 8, 18, 23f., 39, 41, 54,
56, 71, 87f., 91, 95, 98, 105, 109,
111, 121, 123f., 130f., 133, 139f.
Emmerich, H., 189
Enterprise, public, xvi, 31, 51, 66,
87, 102ff., 107, 124f., 164, 167,
180, 189ff.
Enterprise managers, motives and
attitudes of, ix, 56, 143f., 153f.,
157ff., 163, 167, 170, 177f., 183,
187
Enterprise structure, 6, 28, 156
Entrepreneurship, xi, xvii, 15, 47f.,
76, 84, 92, 155ff., 163ff., 180,
187
Executives, selection and training
of, 7, 13, 27ff., 170, 181, 188, 193

Family influences, xv, 4, 6, 22, 28,
31, 50, 53ff., 71, 150ff., 158, 161,
165, 180
Feldman, A. S., 65
Feudal legacy, 2, 15, 176
Fillol, T. R., 68
Financial policies, 83, 85, 108, 121,
129, 133, 140, 146, 164, 173ff.,
183, 190, 192
Foreign role in development, xv,
12, 39, 52, 72, 92, 98, 116ff., 146,
154, 173ff., 184f.
Friedmann, W., 120
Fusfeld, D. R., 47

Galenson, W., 65
Gerschenkron, A., 114
Gonzales, R. F., 120
Gordon, L., 134

Government, economic role of, 14,
25, 47, 51, 55, 61, 71, 78ff., 130,
154, 164ff., 170, 180ff., 184,
189ff.
Grunwald, J., 120
Guatemala, 2, 4, 20f., 34, 41, 61, 64,
71, 79, 91, 94, 106, 111f., 124,
127f., 130, 132f., 139

Harbison, F., 6, 68
Hartmann, H., 155
Heiremans, E., 85
Hirschman, A. O., 87, 166, 182
Hoffman, M. L., 39
Hoselitz, B. F., 156

Incentives, 51, 107f., 154, 170, 180,
183, 188
Indian heritage, xiii, 2, 11, 15, 22,
64, 79, 137, 156
Industrial relations, 44, 53, 67, 120,
176, 183
Industrialization, 9, 33, 44, 48, 79,
89ff., 96, 108, 130, 133, 139f.,
154
Inflation, 10, 69, 74, 91ff., 159, 183
Infrastructure, 81, 104f., 162, 177,
190
Integration, Latin American economic, 41, 48, 91, 124, 136ff.,
175, 194
International Monetary Fund, 100
Investment, xi, 10, 14, 36, 44, 47,
57ff., 70ff., 161, 163, 169
foreign, 116ff., 142, 173ff., 184f.,
192f.

Johnson, John J., 155
Joint international business ventures, 122f., 174, 185

Kalmanoff, G., 120
Keynes, J. M., 96

Lansberg Henríquez, I., 36, 46, 86
Lauterbach, A., 101

Index

Lavin, J. L., 107
Llamazares, J., 58

McClelland, D. C., 85, 155
McMillan, C., Jr., 120
Management, aims of, 42ff., 138
  concepts of, xf., xvi, 15, 26, 56,
    83, 122f., 131, 144ff., 152, 154,
    166, 179ff.
  satisfactions and dissatisfactions,
    48ff., 184
Market size, 4, 40, 57ff., 90, 111, 151,
    157f., 160, 182, 190
Mason, E. S., 135
Medina Echavarría, J., 54, 189
Mexico, 4, 7, 19f., 23, 28ff., 33, 36,
    40, 43ff., 47, 50, 52f., 55, 62ff.,
    66, 68, 71, 73, 77, 80f., 83, 87,
    89ff., 94ff., 98, 102f., 105ff.,
    109ff., 112f., 118ff., 122f., 129,
    131ff., 135, 137ff., 141, 163, 166
Monopoly, 59, 102
Moore, W. E., 65
Myers, C., 6, 65, 68

Nationalism, 20, 24, 29, 53, 112, 120,
    122ff., 139, 174, 184ff.
Neoliberalism, 112f., 168

Organization of American States,
  vi, 194

Paternalism, 15, 54f., 64ff., 70, 184
Personal factors, ix, 30f., 34, 46, 49,
    183
Peru, 4, 12, 14, 79, 156
Planning for development, 80f., 86,
    108f., 133, 146, 156, 167ff., 172,
    180, 186, 190
Political factors, 4, 6, 11, 25, 31, 51,
    81f., 86, 98, 106, 110, 118f., 137,
    159, 161, 170ff., 186
Productivity, 12, 19, 46, 57ff., 69f.,
    98, 162, 182, 184, 190
Profit, xviii, 10f., 44f., 48ff., 50, 56,
    59, 69, 71, 75ff., 121, 151, 157ff.,
    169, 186, 193

Radicalism, 4, 13, 55, 66, 161, 184
Rationalizations, xvi, 24, 37, 54, 108,
    160, 164, 168
Redlich, F., 6
Regional differences, 82, 92, 109
Religious factors, 40, 50, 168
Risk, xi, 47, 75ff., 118, 133, 151, 154,
    156, 161, 183, 189
Roberts, R. S., 32
Ronson, G., 59

Schumpeter, J. A., xi, 76, 84
Short-range view, 10, 15, 75, 136ff.,
    151, 159, 182
Social needs, 4, 11, 22, 46, 50, 66,
    85, 101, 113f., 164, 168
Social setting, 5, 21, 40, 84, 89, 97,
    137, 144
Specialization, lack of, 5, 7, 15
Strassmann, W. P., 155
Sutton, F. X., 192

Tannenbaum, F., 28
Tariffs, 101, 106, 118, 140, 177, 192

United Nations, 84, 127, 194
United States influence, 18, 32, 58,
    64, 70, 77, 92, 101f., 113, 118,
    123, 127ff., 130, 134, 150, 191ff.
Urquidi, V. L., 84
Uruguay, 2, 4, 111, 140
Uslar Pietri, A., 36

Vakil, C. N., 85
Vallenilla, L., 86
Venezuela, 21f., 25, 31f., 34, 36, 38f.,
    43, 45, 52ff., 58, 61, 66, 69, 74,
    80f., 85f., 88, 91, 102, 104, 106,
    109f., 112, 140, 164, 167f., 191
Vernon, R., 83
Vidales, H., 68

Work habits, 11, 21, 55, 61ff., 176,
    184

207